UNIT 2 Jesus Is the Son of God 65

♪ Unit Song • "Blest Are They" 66

CATECHISM PILLARS   CHAPTER   PAGE

WHAT CATHOLICS BELIEVE

5. Jesus, the Image of God **67**
*Jesus shows us how to love others
as God loves us.*

Scripture Story • The Crucifixion **70**

Prayer Celebration • A Prayer of Reflection **74**

Faith in Action   Parish Ministry • Cursillo **76**

HOW CATHOLICS WORSHIP

6. Baptism in Christ **77**
*In Baptism we are united with Christ
and the Church.*

Worship • The Sacrament of Baptism **80**

Prayer Celebration • Our Profession of Faith **84**

Faith in Action   Parish Ministry • Godparents **86**

HOW CATHOLICS LIVE

**7. The Commandments
and the Beatitudes** **87**
*The Beatitudes are paths to happiness
and to God's kingdom.*

Scripture Story • The Beatitudes **90**

Prayer Celebration • A Scripture Prayer **94**

Faith in Action
Parish Ministry • Holy Name Society **96**

HOW CATHOLICS PRAY

**8. The Commandments
and the Kingdom** **97**
*The Ten Commandments and the
Beatitudes lead to God's justice.*

Scripture Story • The Laborers in the Vineyard **100**

Prayer Celebration • A Prayer of Praise **104**

Faith in Action   Parish Ministry • Parish Staff **106**

D0325441

CONTENTS

Let Us Pray 9
Traditional Catholic prayers and devotions

About the Bible 17
Preparing to understand the Scriptures

Program Song 22
"Blest Are We"

UNIT 1 — The Goodness of God 23

♪ Unit Song • "All You Works of God" 24

CHAPTER	PAGE	CATECHISM PILLARS

1. God's Goodness **25**
God reveals himself as One God in Three Persons.

Scripture Story • The Story of Creation 28

Prayer Celebration • A Prayer of Praise 32

Faith in Action — Parish Ministry • Good Stewards 34

WHAT CATHOLICS BELIEVE

2. Praise and Thanksgiving **35**
It is right to give thanks and praise to the Lord our God.

Worship • We Give Thanks and Praise 38

Prayer Celebration • A Prayer of Praise 42

Faith in Action — Parish Ministry • Altar Servers 44

HOW CATHOLICS WORSHIP

3. The Commandments and God's Covenant **45**
The Ten Commandments guide us in serving the one true God.

Scripture Story • Ten Commandments 48

Prayer Celebration • A Prayer of Petition 52

Faith in Action — Parish Ministry • Catechists 54

HOW CATHOLICS LIVE

4. The Commandments and the Lord's Prayer **55**
We follow the message of selflessness by praying the Lord's Prayer.

Scripture Story • The Lord's Prayer 58

Prayer Celebration • Signing the Lord's Prayer 62

Faith in Action — Parish Ministry • Music 64

HOW CATHOLICS PRAY

BLEST ARE WE

Contributing Writers

Ellen Marconi
Faith in Action: Kathleen N. Burke
Feasts and Seasons: Marianne K. Lenihan
Our Catholic Heritage: Joyce A. Crider

Advisory Board

William C. Allegri, M.A., Patricia M. Feeley, S.S.J., M.A.,
Edmund F. Gordon, Patricia A. Hoffmann,
Cris V. Villapando, D.Min.

Consultants

Margaret J. Borders, M.R.S., Kelly O'Lague Dulka, M.S.W.,
Diane Hardick, M.A., Debra Schurko,
Linda S. Tonelli, M.Ed., Joy Villotti-Biedrzycki

Music Advisor

GIA Publications: Michael A. Cymbala, Alec Harris,
Robert W. Piercy

Nihil Obstat

M. Kathleen Flanagan, S.C., Ph.D.
Censor Librorum

Imprimatur

✠ Most Reverend Arthur J. Serratelli
Bishop of Paterson
April 25, 2006

The *nihil obstat* and *imprimatur* are official declarations that a book or pamphlet is free of doctrinal and moral error. No implication is contained therein that those who have granted the *nihil obstat* and *imprimatur* agree with the contents, opinions, or statements expressed.

Acknowledgments

Excerpts from the *New American Bible* with Revised New Testament Copyright © 1986, 1970 Confraternity of Christian Doctrine, Inc., Washington, DC. Used with permission. All rights reserved. No portion of the *New American Bible* may be reprinted without permission in writing from the copyright holder.

All adaptations of Scripture are based on the *New American Bible* with Revised New Testament Copyright © 1986, 1970 Confraternity of Christian Doctrine, Inc., Washington, DC.

Excerpts from the English translation of the *Rite of Marriage* © 1969, International Committee on English in the Liturgy, Inc. (ICEL); excerpts from the English translation of the *Rite of Baptism for Children* © 1969, ICEL; excerpts from the English translation of the *Rite of Penance* © 1974, ICEL; excerpts from the English translation of *Eucharistic Prayers for Masses with Children* © 1975, ICEL; excerpts from the English translation of the *Rite of Confirmation*, Second Edition © 1975, ICEL; excerpts from the English translation of the *Liturgy of the Hours* © 1976, ICEL; excerpts from *Pastoral Care of the Sick: Rites of Anointing and Viaticum* © 1982, ICEL; excerpts from the English translation of *The Roman Missal*, Second Edition © 2010 ICEL; excerpts from the English translation of the *Rite of Christian Initiation of Adults* © 1985, ICEL. All rights reserved.

Music selections copyrighted and/or administered by GIA Publications are used with permission of GIA Publications, Inc., 7404 So. Mason Avenue, Chicago, IL 60638-9927. Please refer to songs for specific copyright dates and information.

In Appreciation: Blessed Kateri Church, Sparta, NJ; Church of the Assumption, Morristown, NJ; Our Lady of Mercy Church, Whippany, NJ; Our Lady of the Lake Church, Sparta, NJ; St. Ann's Church, Parsippany, NJ; St. Joseph's Church, Croton Falls, NY; St. Peter the Apostle Church, Parsippany, NJ; St. Thomas More Church, Convent Station, NJ; GIA Publications, Inc., Chicago, IL; WLP Publications, Franklin Park, IL; Rev. Michael W. Cichon (Sign Language Advisor); Rev. George Hafemann

Excerpts from *Catholic Household Blessings and Prayers* (revised edition) © 2007, United States Conference of Catholic Bishops, Washington, D.C.

Credits

COVER: Gene Plaisted, OSC/The Crosiers

SCRIPTURE ART: Tim Ladwig

ALL OTHER ART: 20–21, 225 Elizabeth Wolf; 26, 28, 36, 46, 50, 56, 58, 70, 78, 88, 90, 98, 100, 110, 112, 120, 130, 132, 140, 154, 172, 174, 196, 204, 214, 216, 224, 226, 228 Tim Ladwig; 30, 40, 72, 102, 166, 198 Roman Dunets; 31, 61, 63, 72, 103, 276, 229 Tom Sperling; 41, 247 Martha Doty; 43, 137 Reggie Holladay; 44, 160 Kelly Kennedy; 48 Scott Cameron; 51, 173 Amanda Harvey; 54, 96, 111, 180, 212 David Helton; 64, 68, 93, 152, 257 Bernadette Lau; 75 Ginna Magee; 79, 167 Bernard Adnet; 99 Morella Fuenmayor; 103 Julie Monks; 115 Freddie Levin; 121 Marion Eldridge; 125 Marcie Hawthorne; 131 Linda Howard Bittner; 135 Jack McMaster; 153, 176, 179 Diana Magnuson; 156 Patti Green; 163, 219 Chris Reed; 166 Gershom Griffith; 195 Sandy Rabinowitz; 209 Terra Muzick; 212, 237 Lauren Cryan; 229 Teresa Berasi; 233, 253 Robin DeWitt; 234 David Bathurst; 241 Jackie Snider; 245 Donna Perrone; 251, 277 Cindy Rosenheim

PHOTOS: Every effort has been made to secure permission and provide appropriate credit for photographic material. The publisher deeply regrets any omission and pledges to correct errors called to its attention in subsequent editions.
3 Chris Sheridan/Catholic New York; 5 Gene Plaisted, OSC/The Crosiers; 7 AP/Wide World; 9 Gene Plaisted, OSC/The Crosiers; 12 ©Richard Cummins/Folio Inc.; 13 Durhan St. Methodist Church, New Zealand/SuperStock; 14 ©Tony Freeman/PhotoEdit; 23 (Bkgd) ©Robert F. Sisson/NGS Image Collection, (Inset) Yavneh Publishing House Ltd.; 26 ©Rob Crandall/The Image Works, Inc.; 27 ©Frank Siteman/Index Stock Imagery; 32 ©Tom Brakefield/Image Works; 36 ©Myrleen Ferguson Cate/PhotoEdit; 38 Chris Sheridan/Catholic New York; 40 ©Rykoff Collection/Corbis; 45 ©William Johnson/Stock Boston; 46 Photofest; 47 ©Mike Brinson/Getty Images; 52 ©Aliki Sapountzi/Aliki Image Library/Alamy Images; 56 (B) ©Morton Beebe, S. F./Corbis, (B) ©Patrick Hertzog/AFP/Getty Images; 57 (B) ©David Young-Wolff/PhotoEdit, (T) ©Lawrence Migdale/Stock Boston; 62 ©Paul Edmondson/Getty Images; 65 (Bkgd) ©Sonia Halliday Photographs, (Inset) Bridgeman Art; 68 ©Richard Barenholtz/Corbis; 69 William Zdinak, Artist; 72 (CR) Sarah Johnson, (BR) June Jamison Thorne; 73 (T) ©David Young-Wolff/PhotoEdit, (B) ©John Welzenbach/Corbis; 74 (B) ©Richard Hutchings/PhotoEdit, (Bkgd) ©William Waterfall/Pacific Stock; 79 ©Myrleen Ferguson Cate/PhotoEdit; 83 Jim Whitmer; 84 (L) Richard Lord, (Bkgd) ©Bob Daemmrich/Stock Boston; 88 Sean Sprague/©CNEWA, NY; 89 ©Bill Wittman; 92 Corbis; 94 ©H. David Seawell/Corbis; 107 (Bkgd, Inset) ©Sonia Halliday Photographs; 110 ©The Art Archive/Corbis; 116 ©Stefano Amantini/Atlantide/Bruce Coleman Inc.; 121 ©Myrleen Ferguson Cate/PhotoEdit; 122 Gene Plaisted, OSC/The Crosiers; 126 ©David Young-Wolff/PhotoEdit; 129 ©R. Barry Levy/Index Stock Imagery; 130 Little Sisters of the Poor; 134 The Nicholas Green Foundation/Sculpted and designed by Bruce Hasson; 136 ©E. R. Degginger/Bruce Coleman Inc.; 139 (R) ©Mary Kate Denny/Getty Images, (L) Jim Cummins; 140 GIA Publications; 141 (B) ©Tom McCarthy/Photri, Inc., (T) Gene Plaisted, OSC/The Crosiers; 146 (Inset) Myrleen Cate, (Bkgd) Index Stock Imagery; 149 (Bkgd) ©Richard T. Nowitz, (Inset) ©The British Museum/DK Images; 152 Joe Rimkus, Jr./Catholic News Service; 158 (Inset) ©Arthur Tilley/Getty Images, (Bkgd) SuperStock; 162 ©Francis G. Mayer/Corbis; 168 ©John Shaw/Bruce Coleman Inc.; 172 The Printery House of Conception Abbey; 178 (Bkgd) ©Thomas Winz/Panoramic Images, (Inset) ©Myrleen Ferguson Cate/PhotoEdit; 182 ©Brooks Kraft/Corbis; 191 (Bkgd) ©Sonia Halliday Photographs, (Inset) ©Erich Lessing/Art Resource, NY; 194 Scala/Art Resource, NY; 198 The Granger Collection, NY; 199 (L) ©Bill Wittman, (R) James L. Shaffer; 200 ©Bonnie Kamin/PhotoEdit; 204 ©Franco Origlia/Getty Images; 205 ©Bill Horsman/Stock Boston; 206 AP/Wide World; 208 ©Stephen R. Swan/Canstock Images, Inc./Index Stock Imagery; 210 (T, Bkgd) Gene Plaisted, OSC/The Crosiers, (C) The Cummer Museum of Art and Gardens, Jacksonville, Florida/SuperStock; 210 Gene Plaisted, OSC/The Crosiers; 214 Everett Collection, Inc.; 218 ©Bettmann/Corbis; 220 ©Robert Frerck/Stone; 224 Musée d'Orsay, Paris, France/Erich Lessing/Art Resource, NY; 225 ©Peter Turnley/Corbis; 230 ©Ed Honowitz/Getty Images; 238 Corbis; 240 Fr. Carl B. Trutter, O.P.; 243 ©Dorothy Greco/Image Works; 244 Jim Whitmer; 246 SuperStock; 249 CLEO; 252 (T) ©Myrleen Ferguson Cate/PhotoEdit, (B) ©Bill Wittman; 254 ©Bill Wittman; 255 ©Lawrence Migdale/Stock Boston; 256 Richard Lord; 258 Galleria Palatina, Palazzo Pitti, Florence, Italy/Scala/Art Resource, NY; 263 Gene Plaisted, OSC/The Crosiers; 264 Gene Plaisted, OSC/The Crosiers; 265 ©Bill Wittman; 270 ©Mary Kate Denny/PhotoEdit; 273 ©Myrleen Cate/Index Stock Imagery

FAITH & WORD EDITION
✝ BLEST ARE WE

Faith comes from what is heard,
and what is heard comes through the word of Christ.

Romans 10:17

Series Authors

Rev. Richard N. Fragomeni, Ph.D.
Maureen Gallagher, Ph.D.
Jeannine Goggin, M.P.S.
Michael P. Horan, Ph.D.

Scripture Co-editor and Consultant
Maria Pascuzzi, S.S.L., S.T.D.

Multicultural Consultant
Angela Erevia, M.C.D.P., M.R.E.

This book reflects the
new revision of the

ROMAN MISSAL

THIRD EDITION

RCL ✝ Benziger®

Cincinnati, Ohio

A **Match** column A with column B by writing the correct number in the space provided.

A

1. The _Blessed Sacrament_ is another name for the Eucharist kept in the tabernacle.

2. A tabernacle is a container in church where the Blessed Sacrament is kept for those unable to come to _Mass_ due to illness or for private prayer.

3. Jesus obeyed the Ten _Commandments_ by loving others.

4. _Prayer_ helps us accept God's plan for each of us.

5. Mary is a _model_ of faith.

B

_4_ prayer

_1_ Blessed Sacrament

_5_ model

_2_ Mass

_3_ Commandments

B **Circle** the letter of the best answer.

1. In the Scripture story, who did Jesus say is part of his family?
   a. the Twelve Apostles
   b. Mary and Joseph
   c. people who do what God asks
   d. people who know the Commandments

2. The _____ Commandment helps us to keep healthy and respect the life and health of others.
   a. First
   b. Fifth
   c. Sixth
   d. Fourth

3. The _d_ Commandment teaches us to listen to our parents.
   a. First
   b. Fifth
   c. Sixth
   d. Fourth

4. The _____ Commandment helps us respect our bodies and the bodies and privacy of others.
   a. First
   b. Fifth
   c. Sixth
   d. Fourth

Faith in Action

Eucharistic Holy Hour Ministry From the time of Christ's birth, people came to worship and adore him. Just before his death, he asked his disciples to stay with him and to watch and pray. Catholics today can spend time with Jesus in silent prayer before the Blessed Sacrament. In a Holy Hour, we can find peace in our hearts as we pray silently. We also listen during these times of quiet to what Christ wants to say to us. He speaks to us in the silence and through Scripture readings and songs. God knows what is in our hearts, even before we speak.

In Everyday Life

Activity Good friends don't always use words to communicate. Describe a time when you have enjoyed some quiet time, just being with someone you care about.

_____

_____

_____

In Your Parish

Activity A Holy Hour is an opportunity to spend time in the presence of Jesus Christ in the Blessed Sacrament. Place a ✔ next to the things or people you would like to include if you were participating in a Holy Hour.

___ silent prayer time

___ prayers to read silently

___ a basket of written prayer requests

___ songs

___ my parents

___ pray the Rosary

___ Scripture readings

___ my friends

___ the Blessed Sacrament

___ the parish staff

The Church

The Church spread rapidly in the first century. Disciples such as Saint Paul preached the Gospel and established communities around the Mediterranean world. These churches became centers of a new sense of justice and worship.

We are all baptized into one Body.
Based on 1 Corinthians 12:13

Some of Paul's letters to Christian communities were sent by messenger along this ancient Roman road. Paul wrote his letters with a reed pen dipped in a pot of black ink.

Hands of Healing

FAMILY TIME

Sacraments in the Church

The Seven Sacraments speak largely to our vocation as Christians. In Baptism we accept the calling of being a Christian. In Confirmation we are sealed in that calling. The Eucharist gives us the strength to live in Christ. Penance and Reconciliation helps us keep our path clear for living out our vocation. In the Sacrament of the Anointing of the Sick, through Jesus Christ, the Church heals our infirmities. Matrimony and Holy Orders are two ways we can live out this vocation. Receiving the Sacraments helps us to be better Christians.

ACTIVITY

Sacramental Signs God uses ordinary things such as bread, water, and oil in extraordinary ways. They transform our lives and communicate his love for us. Ask family members to share signs that communicate to them that they are loved.

WEEKLY PLANNER

On Sunday

Remember that the Eucharistic celebration makes present the life, Death, and Resurrection of Jesus Christ.

On the Web

www.blestarewe.com

Visit our Web site for the saint of the day and the reflection question of the week.

Saint of the Week

Saint Rose Philippine Duchesne (1769–1852)

Born in France, Rose eventually became a Missionary of the Sacred Heart and came to the United States. She opened the first free school for girls and founded six convents along the Mississippi River. Saint Rose died at St. Charles, Missouri, in 1852.

Patron Saint of: diocese of Springfield-Cape Girardeau, Missouri

Feast Day: November 18

A Prayer for the Week

Dear God, your saving grace surrounds us. We remember Saint Rose's mission of spreading your grace to others. We are thankful for your love and grace that are shared in the sacraments. Amen.

FAMILY TIME

✝ Scripture Background

In the Early Church

Corinth   During the first century, many people passed through the city of Corinth in Greece. Merchants stopped at this busy seaport when traveling between Rome and Asia Minor. The city was well-known throughout the Mediterranean world as a commercial center. Unfortunately, Corinth was also known for its corruption and immorality. Paul took on the challenge of establishing a church in this prosperous city. After he left the city, Paul continued to guide the Christian community through his writings.

Read his letter in 1 Corinthians 12:12–26.

OUR CATHOLIC TRADITION in Music

One Body In Christ

Receiving the Eucharist reawakens the love of Christ in us and makes us more loving toward others. In 1993, Irish Catholic composer Dana sang the song "We Are One Body" at the World Youth Day ceremonies in Denver, Colorado. She composed this song to remind the thousands of teens and young adults in attendance that we are "one Body in Christ."

Dana singing "We Are One Body" at World Youth Day, 1993

13 Sacraments in the Church

LET US PRAY

We are all baptized into one Body.

Based on 1 Corinthians 12:13

Share

As Christians, we believe that every person is an important member of God's family. We must work together to bring God's goodness to everyone.

Activity

Team Spirit

Choose who will play the following roles and act out the story.

Narrator: At St. Joseph's parish picnic, a group of girls decide to play volleyball. As they are about to begin a game, Ashleigh comes over to join them.

Ashleigh: "Can I play on a team?"

Narrator: No one answers. Everyone knows Ashleigh does not run very fast. After a while Juanita agrees to let Ashleigh on her team. She tries to help Ashleigh whenever she cannot get to the ball fast enough.

Juanita: "I'll help you, Ashleigh."

Narrator: When it is Ashleigh's turn to serve, she hits the ball really hard and scores a point for her team. Juanita and the others cheer her on. They shout . . .

The Team: "Way to go!"

How do members of the Christian family work together?

Hear & Believe

✝ Scripture   One Body, Many Parts

Our Church carries out Christ's mission in the world. Christ's mission is to bring the Kingdom of God to all people. Every person has talents that help spread God's peace and love to the world. Saint Paul understood that it was necessary that all members of the Church work together. When he wrote to the Christians in the city of Corinth, Paul compared the Body of Christ to a human body.

A body is one, but it has many parts. It needs all its parts: feet, eyes, ears, everything to work. For example, the body has eyes. Is the ear a part of the body even if it is not an eye? Yes! The body needs hearing as well as sight. It is the same with Christ and his Church. Together, we make up the Body of Christ. No matter who we are, we are all baptized into one Body, the Church.

Based on 1 Corinthians 12:12–26

Sharing the Life of Jesus

The Church is a community of people united with God and with each other. Through Jesus Christ, the Church heals the sick and helps those who are poor and hungry. In doing this we carry out Christ's mission in the world. Together we lead all people closer to God's kingdom.

By the power of the Holy Spirit, Jesus Christ is present when the Church celebrates the **Sacraments**. The Seven Sacraments were instituted by Christ to fill us with grace. Grace strengthens us in carrying out his mission and the mission of the Church. We celebrate the Sacraments in the Catholic community as a sign that grace comes to us through the Church, united with the Body of Christ.

GO TO pages 262–265 to read more about the Sacraments.

Our Church Teaches

We celebrate the Sacraments to help us love others as Jesus loved us. Christ's presence in the Church is called a mystery. We do not see Jesus in person, yet we know he lives through the Church.

The Church encourages us to receive the Sacraments so that we can be united with Jesus. By leading a Christian life, we move closer to being in God's kingdom forever.

We Believe

The Church celebrates the Sacraments so that we can fully experience Christ's loving presence. Together with the whole Church, we can carry out Christ's mission in the world.

Faith Words

Body of Christ
The Body of Christ is the People of God or the Church.

Sacraments
Sacraments are sacred signs that celebrate God's love for us and Christ's presence in our lives and in the Church.

What are the Seven Sacraments?

Respond

We Are Living the Sacraments

When we celebrate the Sacraments, we are united in Christ.

Activities

1. Discover the hidden message by coloring the spaces as marked.
   Diamonds: green. Stars: red. Circles: blue.

2. Complete the following sentence.

   I know Christ lives in me because _____

   _____

   _____

   _____ .

3. Look at the crossword puzzle below. Use the clues to fill in the name for the Sacrament being described.

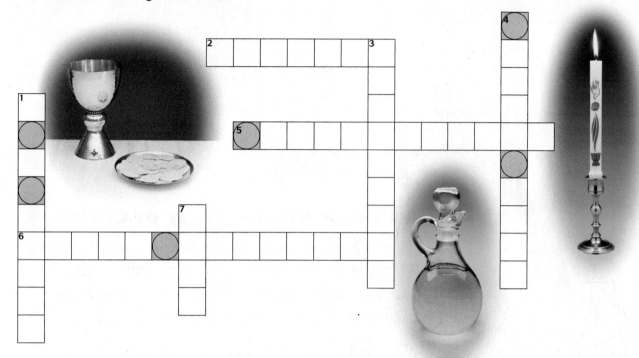

Across

2. We begin a new life as members of the Church.

5. We are sealed with the Gift of the Holy Spirit.

6. Christ forgives our sins.

Down

1. The Body and Blood of Christ nourish us.

3. A man and a woman promise to be faithful to one another.

4. Bishops, priests, and deacons promise to share in Jesus' work.

7. Christ heals and strengthens those who are ill in the Sacrament of the Anointing of the _____.

4. Write the letters that are circled in the crossword puzzle.

Letters _____

Unscramble them to complete this sentence.

The __ __ __ __ __ __ celebrates the Seven Sacraments.

What can we do as members of the Body of Christ?

✝ Prayer Celebration

A Prayer for the Body of Christ

(Turn to page 154 and read the Scripture passage again. When you are finished, complete each sentence to tell how you can help others. Two have been done for you. Then share your answers with a partner.)

With my hands, I can reach out to others.

With my eyes, I can _____.

With my head, I can _____.

With my ears, I can _____.

With my feet, I can _____.

With my whole body, I can carry out Christ's mission in the world.

13 Chapter Review

A Complete the sentences with words from the box.

Christ's mission	grace	body
Sacraments	mystery	Church

1. Sacred signs that celebrate Christ's presence in our lives are called _Sacraments_.

2. Saint Paul used the image of a _body_ to show how Christians work together to spread God's goodness.

3. The Body of Christ is the People of God or the _Church_.

4. When we spread God's peace and love to others we are carrying out _Christ's mission_.

5. Christ's presence in the Church is called a _Mystery_.

B Match column A with column B by writing the correct number in the space provided.

A		B
1. Baptism	_5_	receive God's grace when we are sick.
2. Confirmation	_1_	become a member of the Body of Christ.
3. Eucharist	_3_	receive the Body and Blood of Christ.
4. Peanance and Reconciliation	_7_	promise to do God's work as a priest, bishop, or deacon.
5. Anointing of the Sick	_2_	sealed with the Gift of the Holy Spirit.
6. Matrimony	_4_	receive God's forgiveness.
7. Holy Orders	_6_	promise to be faithful in marriage.

Faith in Action

The Parish Liturgy Committee   Another word for the Mass is "liturgy," which means "the work of the people." People work behind the scenes to help us pray when we come together as a faith community. They help us celebrate the seasons of the Church year, such as Advent and Lent, by decorating the church and working with the parish music ministers. They may also write the Prayer of the Faithful. They help us love and understand Scripture. They teach people to share in the many sacramental ministries and give us opportunities to take part in celebrating the Sacraments.

In Your Parish

Activity   Either alone or as a group, write your own Prayer of the Faithful. Decide how you want everyone to respond after each petition.

Prayer response: _____.

For our parish leaders, especially, _____

_____. We pray to the Lord.

For those in our parish and families, who are sick or dying, especially

_____. We pray to the Lord.

In Everyday Life

Activity   Think about the next special event on your family's celebration calendar, such as a birthday. List the jobs that will need to be done before or at the celebration and who will complete each task. More than one person can be named for each task.

TO DO

what   who

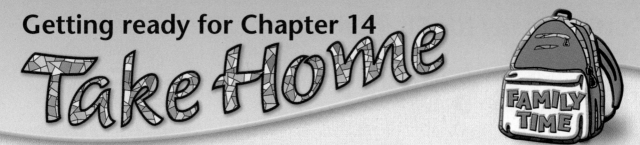

The Sacrament of Reconciliation

Learning to say "I'm sorry" and learning to say "You're forgiven" are two important lessons that families pass on to their children. Some people find it very difficult to ask for or seek forgiveness. Others find it easy to say the words but don't really understand the meaning behind them. The Church gives us a wonderful opportunity to experience God's forgiveness in the Sacrament of Penance and Reconciliation.

ACTIVITY

Forgiveness Chart Write the name of each person in your family on a sheet of paper. Keep a record this week of how many times you have a disagreement with each person by placing a mark next to that person's name. Cross out the mark when you or the person who hurt you says, "I'm sorry."

Forgiveness Chart
Tom ☒ ☒ ☒ ☒
Georganne ☒ ☐
Ted ☒
Joan ☒ ☒
Bill ☐

WEEKLY PLANNER

On Sunday

During the Penitential Act, pray in a special way for those in your family who can't let go of their anger.

On the Web

www.blestarewe.com

Visit our Web site for the saint of the day and the reflection question of the week.

Saint of the Week

Saint John Vianney
(1786–1859)

Saint John Vianney was a French priest. His study for the priesthood was extremely difficult for him and he was eventually ordained because of his good will. He was sent to a poor, remote parish, where he served for forty years.

Patron Saint of: parish clergy
Feast Day: August 4

A Prayer for the Week

Lord, learning can be so demanding at times. Lift us up, Lord, and encourage us. Like Saint John Vianney, may we continue to learn how to forgive others as you have forgiven us.
Amen.

Take Home

FAMILY TIME

✚ Scripture Background

In the Early Church

Confession Early Christians who committed serious crimes such as murder or adultery had to confess their sins and do public penance. Often their act of penance lasted for years. Beginning in the seventh century, confessions became private. Irish missionaries introduced this practice, which allowed for the priest to forgive mortal and venial sins in Christ's name. In the sixteenth century, small rooms called confessionals became a common sight in Catholic churches.

In the Gospels we learn that Jesus often forgave sins. Read Matthew 9:1–8.

OUR CATHOLIC TRADITION in Literature

Confessions Saint Augustine is a saint whose story reveals a sinner who turned to the Lord and turned away from sin. After living a worldly life, he converted to Catholicism at the age of thirty-three. He became one of the most important voices the Church has ever heard. His autobiographical book, entitled *Confessions*, contains the famous quote about searching for God: "You have made us for yourself, and our heart is restless until it rests in you."

Saint Augustine, 14th–16th century, San Gimignano, Italy

14 The Sacrament of Reconciliation

Give thanks to the Lord for he is good.
His mercy endures forever.

Based on the Rite of Penance

Share

God wants us to be kind and loving. Sometimes we forget that our words and actions affect those around us. If we make selfish choices, then we hurt the people we are with.

Activity

Tell how the entire family is hurt by the actions of the two children.

_____

_____

_____

_____

_____

How do we receive God's forgiveness?

Hear & Believe

Worship Jesus Forgives Sins

Through the Sacrament of **Penance and Reconciliation**, Jesus gave the Church the power to forgive **sin**. When we are sorry for our sins, we can receive this Sacrament. The Sacrament of Penance and Reconciliation heals our relationship with God, the Church, and one another.

Mortal Sin and Venial Sin

When we sin, we turn away from God and the way God wants us to live. A **mortal sin** is a serious sin that separates us from God's grace. To commit a mortal sin, a person must do something that is very wrong, understand that it is wrong, and do it anyway. A **venial sin** is a less serious sin. Our Church teaches us that all sin hurts our relationship with God and one another.

Celebrating God's Love and Forgiveness

We can celebrate the Sacrament of Penance and Reconciliation alone with the priest or as a community with private confession. A communal celebration helps us understand that our individual sins affect the entire Christian community.

Forgiveness from God

In the special prayer of **absolution**, we are reconciled with God and the Church.

God, the Father of mercies,
through the death and Resurrection of his Son
has reconciled the world to himself
and sent the Holy Spirit among us
for the forgiveness of sins;
through the ministry of the Church,
may God give you pardon and peace,
and I absolve you from your sins
in the name of the Father, and of the Son,
and of the Holy Spirit.
Amen.

Rite of Penance

Giving Thanks

Before the celebration of the Sacrament is finished, we pray the following prayer of thanksgiving.

Give thanks to the Lord, for he is good.
His mercy endures forever.

Based on the Rite of Penance

 page 269 to read more about the Sacrament of Penance and Reconciliation.

Our Church Teaches

While he was on Earth, Jesus showed us his healing power. The Church celebrates the **Sacraments of Healing** today, bringing us Jesus' strength and peace.

Our sins affect our relationship with God and the entire Christian community. God forgives us through the Sacrament of Penance and Reconciliation. We are reunited with God and the Church and promise to reject sin. We are grateful to God for this special gift.

We Believe

Through the Sacrament of Penance and Reconciliation, our relationship with God and the Church is healed.

Faith Words

mortal sin
A mortal sin is a serious violation of God's law. It separates us from God's grace until we ask for forgiveness in the Sacrament of Penance and Reconciliation.

venial sin
A venial sin is a less serious sin. It weakens our love for God and others and can lead to mortal sin.

absolution
Through the prayer of absolution, the priest forgives our sins in the name of God.

How do we bring God's forgiveness to others?

Respond

Saint John Vianney Brought God's Forgiveness to Others

 Saint John Vianney hoped to be a priest so he could bring Christ's love and forgiveness to others. He was born near Lyons, France, in 1786. As a boy, he worked on his father's farm. With the help of the local pastor, John studied to become a priest. It was difficult for him to learn. He attended school for only a year, but kept trying to leave. He was ordained a priest at the age of twenty-nine.

It was as a priest that John's gifts and talents became clear. He worked in a small town with only about 200 people living in it. The people loved to hear John preach, and he soon became known throughout Europe.

Crowds started lining up early in the morning to celebrate the Sacrament of Reconciliation with John. People said that John Vianney knew things that they didn't even tell him. With a few simple words, he comforted them and brought them closer to God.

We remember Saint John Vianney's life as a priest and the way he brought God's forgiveness to others. The Church celebrates his feast day on August 4.

Activity

Imagine that you are teaching someone the steps for receiving the Sacrament of Penance and Reconciliation. Look at the chart below. Complete the directions for the steps of the Sacrament of Reconciliation.

1. Preparation

   Write one question that could be used to help you examine your conscience.

   _____

2. Priest's Welcome

3. Reading from Scripture

   Write the name of a reading from the Bible that could be used.

   _____

4. Confession

   Give an example of a kind act or a prayer that the priest might give as penance.

   _____

5. Prayer of Sorrow

   Write your own prayer of sorrow.

   _____

   _____

   _____

6. Absolution

7. Prayer of Praise and Dismissal

   Write your own prayer of praise. Thank God for the gift of Reconciliation.

   _____

   _____

How do we know if we are living according to God's will?

✝ Prayer Celebration

An Examination of Conscience

Leader: Our relationship with God is the most important thing in our lives. God wants us to remain close to him and to share his love with others. Let us now examine our conscience to see if we are living according to God's will.

Reader 1: Do I pray often so I can be close to God?

Reader 2: Do I thank God for my family and friends and all his gifts of creation?

Reader 3: Do I use the talents God gave me to help others?

Reader 4: Do I share what I have with others?

Reader 5: Do I forgive others when they hurt me?

Reader 6: Do I help bring peace to my school and my community?

Reader 7: Do I always try to do the right thing, even when it is difficult?

All: God loves us and is always ready to forgive our sins.

(Share a sign of peace with each other.)

14 Chapter Review

A Circle the letter of the best answer.

1. A _____ sin is a serious sin that separates us from God's grace.
   a. venial
   b. minor
   c. mortal
   d. strong

2. A sin that weakens a person's love for others is called a _____.
   a. venial sin
   b. small sin
   c. serious sin
   d. mortal sin

3. When a priest prays the prayer of _____, we are reconciled with God and the Church.
   a. thanksgiving
   b. praise
   c. absolution
   d. petition

4. When we make selfish choices we _____ God and the entire Christian community.
   a. hurt
   b. help
   c. love
   d. reconcile

B Respond to the following questions.

1. How did Saint John Vianney bring God's forgiveness to others?

_____

_____

_____

_____

2. How do you feel after you receive Jesus' forgiveness?

_____

_____

_____

_____

_____

Faith in Action

Anointing of the Sick and Ministry to the Infirmed For many years, Catholics received the Sacrament of the Anointing of the Sick only when they were very old or so ill that they might soon die. Today, we can experience the strengthening of this Sacrament any time we need healing. The Sacrament can include prayers for healing, anointing of our bodies with the Oil of the Sick, and the laying on of hands. We can all share in the ministry of healing by praying for the sick and for their families. When people are afraid or discouraged, we can encourage them with prayers for strength and peace.

In Everyday Life

Activity Think about a time when you were sick. Place a ✔ next to the things that people did for you during for this time. Which of these can you do for someone else who is sick? Share your answers with a partner.

___ Prayed for me   ___ Visited me   ___ Brought me homework

___ Held my hand   ___ Cheered me up   ___ Made my favorite meal

___ Sent get well cards   ___ Helped me stop worrying   ___ Other (describe)

In Your Parish

Activity Identify four people in your parish or family who need healing. Suggest one way that you and your friends could offer comfort to each person.

Name	How we can help
1. _____	_____
2. _____	_____
3. _____	_____
4. _____	_____

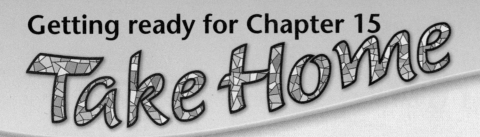

FAMILY TIME

The Commandments and Forgiveness

Sin is a concern for the Church because it not only separates us from God's grace, it also affects all of our relationships. When we sin, we choose our wishes over what God asks of us. Reconciliation restores a sense of peace with God and with others, especially with those close to us.

ACTIVITY

How Was Your Day? During this week, spend a few minutes with your child each night to review his or her day. Ask your child to list all the things that he or she liked about the day and then ask if there were any disappointments. It is a good time for each of you to express sorrow for the things that went wrong. Together you can ask for God's forgiveness and help to make tomorrow better.

WEEKLY PLANNER

On Sunday

Listen to the Scripture readings and homily at Mass to discover guidance for leading a moral life.

On the Web

www.blestarewe.com

Visit our Web site for the saint of the day and the reflection question of the week.

Saint of the Week

Saint Matilda
(c. 895–968)

Saint Matilda was a German queen during the tenth century. Her sons fought among themselves and were jealous when Matilda was generous to the poor and the Church. She died with a great reputation for kindness and generosity among people.

Patron Saint of: large families, the falsely accused

Feast Day: March 14

A Prayer for the Week

Dear Lord, forgive us for the times we have failed to love you and for the times we have hurt others. Help us to be like Saint Matilda by being kind and generous towards those we meet. Amen.

Take Home

FAMILY TIME

✝ Scripture Background

Before the Time of Jesus

Inheritance   In ancient times, the Israelites considered the land of Canaan as their inheritance from God. They valued the land and passed it on from generation to generation. Sons were first in line to inherit land as well as other property such as household goods and cattle. The oldest son usually received a greater share, since he was responsible for his mother and unmarried sisters.

In Luke 15:11–20, a son seeks forgiveness for wasting his inheritance.

OUR CATHOLIC TRADITION in Art

Icons   Icons are colorful paintings of Jesus, Mary, and the saints that help us pray. They are usually painted directly on flat surfaces such as the wall of a church or on wood panels or screens that are often placed at the front of a church. In the Eastern Catholic Church, icons serve the same function as statues do in the Western Catholic Church. Icons are not signed by the artist who paints them because they are visual prayers that reflect God's goodness and glory.

Icon of the Prodigal Son

15 The Commandments and Forgiveness

LET US PRAY For we have sinned against you.

Penitential Act of the Mass

Share

Sometimes people may disappoint or hurt us. God calls us to forgive them so that we can continue to grow in God's love.

Activity

Circle the set of pictures that shows forgiveness.

How does God show us forgiveness?

Hear & Believe

✝ Scripture The Forgiving Father

Jesus often taught with stories. One day he told this story to explain God's great love and forgiveness.

A man had two sons. The younger son asked for the money his father would leave him in his will so that he could leave home. He then moved far away and did not live a good or healthy life. Soon he had no money and was always hungry. "I would be living better if I were working for my father!" the son thought. "I will go home, ask my father for forgiveness, and tell him how sorry I am." So he started to walk home.

While the son was still a long way off, his father saw him coming. The father ran to his son and hugged him. The son said, "Father, I have sinned against God and you. I do not deserve to be called your son." But his father was not angry. He told his servants to give him beautiful clothes and sandals and prepare a special meal. Seeing all of this, the older brother became angry.

"Father, I have always done what you asked, and yet you never had a celebration for me. But my brother, who wasted your money, gets a wonderful feast like this?" the older son complained.

The father said, "You are with me always. All that I have is yours. But we have to celebrate because your brother was dead to us and has come back to life. He was lost and has now been found."

Based on Luke 15:11–32

Our Conscience

God calls us always to choose what is good. We are responsible for the choices we make. Our **conscience** helps us to know what is good. It is guided by what the Church teaches about God's Laws, especially the Ten Commandments.

Our conscience tells us how our actions will affect our relationship with God and others. To make good **moral decisions**, we must pray, learn the teachings of the Church, and follow our conscience.

Even when we sin, God continues to speak to each of us through our conscience. When we are sorry, God is ready to forgive us, especially in the Sacrament of Reconciliation. As the story of the forgiving father reminds us, we can always come back to God's love.

Understanding the 7th, 8th, 9th, and 10th Commandments

The Seventh through Tenth Commandments teach us to treat others in loving and unselfish ways. The Seventh Commandment teaches us that we must respect the property of others and that we should never take what doesn't belong to us. The Eighth Commandment teaches us to be honest and truthful.

In the Scripture story of the forgiving father, the younger son was very selfish. The Ninth and Tenth Commandments teach us not to be selfish, envious, or jealous. Instead we should be thankful to God for all the gifts he has given us.

Our Church Teaches

Sin hurts our relationship with God and others as well as ourselves. God helps us avoid sin by speaking to our conscience. Our conscience is our inner self, guided by God. Our conscience also directs us to heal our relationships with God and with each other.

We Believe

Our conscience helps us to love and forgive others. It is guided by what the Church teaches about God's Laws, especially the Ten Commandments.

Faith Words

conscience
Our conscience is our ability to know what is right and what is wrong. God speaks to us in our conscience and helps us make responsible decisions.

moral decisions
Moral decisions are choices between what is good and what is wrong.

How can we make good moral decisions?

Respond

Three Steps to Making a Good Moral Decision

1. **Stop and think about your situation.**

   Ask: What do I want to do or say? Is it right or wrong?

2. **Consider what you have learned about Jesus and the Church.**

   Ask: How will my choice affect others? Will my words or actions help or hurt someone?

3. **Think what is best for you.**

   Ask: Am I being pressured by my friends to do this? Am I afraid to do the right thing?

Activities

1. Read the story. Then answer the questions, using the three steps above as a guide.

   Rick told his friend Jack he would go to his bowling party. Later, he received an invitation from Joey to attend his party at the movie theater. It is the same day as Jack's party.

   Rick really wants to see the new movie that everyone is talking about at school. Rick is thinking about skipping Jack's party and going to the movies instead. Joey said that Rick should tell Jack he was not feeling well and that he will have to miss his bowling party.

   a. Would it be right or wrong for Rick to miss Jack's party?

   _____

   _____

   b. What has Rick been taught?

   _____

   _____

   c. Should Rick listen to Joey? Why or why not?

   _____

   _____

   _____

2. As the forgiving father did in the story, God will always love us. He wants us to mend our relationships with others. Think about how your conscience would guide you in the following situations. Write or draw an ending to each story.

Have faith and a good conscience.

Based on 1 Timothy 1:19

Your friend starts using your video game without asking permission. Your conscience tells you to…

_____

_____

_____

You have an argument with your parents when they don't give you permission to go out with your friends. Your conscience tells you to…

_____

_____

_____

How do we pray for God's forgiveness?

Prayer Celebration

A Prayer for Forgiveness

Leader: At Mass and other special times, we ask God to forgive our sins. We pray for his mercy. Let us pause and reflect on the things we are not happy we did. Also, think about the good things we failed to do.

Leader: Lord, we have sinned against you: Lord, have mercy.

All: Lord, have mercy.

Leader: Show us, O Lord, your mercy.

All: And grant us your salvation.

All: May God bless us, protect us, and bring us to everlasting life. Amen.

Leader: Let us now offer each other a sign of peace.

Based on the Penitential Act of the Mass and the Liturgy of the Hours

A **Match** column A with column B by writing the correct number in the space provided.

A

1. Seventh

2. Eighth

3. Ninth

4. conscience

5. moral decisions

B

_3_ and Tenth Commandments teach us not to be selfish.

___ our ability to know what is right and what is wrong.

_2_ Commandment teaches us to be honest and truthful.

___ the choices between what is good and what is wrong.

_1_ Commandment teaches that we must respect the property of others.

B **Circle** the number of each question you should ask yourself when faced with a difficult decision.

1. What do I want to do or say?

2. Will my actions help me to be popular?

3. Am I being pressured by my friends to do this?

4. What is the easier thing to do?

5. How will my choice affect others?

6. How can I do it without getting into trouble?

Faith in Action

The Parish Pastoral Council Since your pastor is only one person, he can best lead and serve the parish with the help of others. Using their eyes to see and their ears to listen, members of the Parish Pastoral Council advise the pastor and help him understand and meet the needs of all the people in the parish. Together, they listen to the Holy Spirit. The council help the pastor set goals for the parish that will help everyone to know how caring and loving a parish family can be. Sometimes they summarize these goals in a mission statement.

In Everyday Life

Activity What should the boy do or say? On the lines below, write a caption that best describes the scene.

_____

_____

_____

_____

_____

In Your Parish

Activity Conduct a survey in your group to find out what children your age think they can do to help meet some of the needs they see and hear in the parish family. You may want to then put your ideas in writing to the Parish Pastoral Council.

To the members of _____ Parish Pastoral Council,

_____

_____

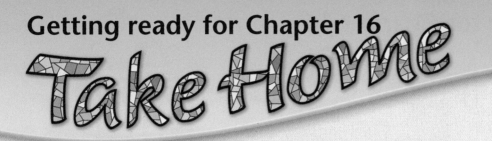

The Commandments and Praying for Forgiveness

The Bible tells of God's great love for us. The writers, inspired by the Holy Spirit, tell stories about God's creation of the world. One story is about Adam and Eve. God gave them the gift of free will. The Bible says that because Adam and Eve used that gift to reject God's love, Jesus was sent to redeem their descendants from sin and death.

ACTIVITY

A Place of Honor If your family has a copy of the Bible, put it where you and your child can see it each day. The Bible will be read more often if it is readily seen. If you do not own one, plan to purchase a copy. Ask your DRE or catechist at your parish for suggestions.

WEEKLY PLANNER

On Sunday

During the Lord's Prayer, recall the times you have failed to live according to God's will. Ask for forgiveness.

On the Web

www.blestarewe.com

Visit our Web site for the saint of the day and the reflection question of the week.

Saint of the Week

Blessed Mariana of Jesus (1565–1624)

At age 23, Blessed Mariana of Jesus became a discalced (without shoes) Mercedarian nun in Madrid. She is remembered for her life of penance, devotion to the Eucharist, and intense prayer life. She is also known as the "Lily of Madrid."

Feast Day: April 27

A Prayer for the Week

Lord, we are thankful for your unending love. Help us to follow the example of Blessed Mariana by remembering the need to forgive as we have been forgiven. Amen.

Take Home

FAMILY TIME

✝ Scripture Background

Before the Time of Jesus

Loans   In biblical times, it was considered a good deed to lend to people in need. To secure a loan, the borrower had to pledge something such as his land or animals. Sometimes a borrower might even pledge a family member. If the loan was not repaid, the promised relative became a slave to the lender. Every seventh year, all debts were cancelled and these slaves were freed.

In Matthew 18:21–35, Jesus teaches forgiveness through the parable of the king who cancels the debt of his servant.

OUR CATHOLIC TRADITION in Social Justice

Dead Man Walking

Sister Helen Prejean, a Sister of Saint Joseph, lives in Louisiana and works with prisoners awaiting the death penalty. She recounts her efforts to spare a murderer from being executed in the book and film *Dead Man Walking*. Both the book and the movie center on forgiveness from and reconciliation with God.

16 The Commandments and Praying for Forgiveness

Forgive your brothers and sisters from your heart.

Based on Matthew 18:35

Share

Lorraine and Angela had a fight. Angela was telling untrue stories about Lorraine to their friend Dominick. She told Lorraine that she was sorry and promised not to do it again. Although Lorraine was upset, she forgave Angela. A little while later, Angela's brother, Frank, told her that he broke her favorite CD and was very sorry. Angela got angry and yelled at Frank. She said she couldn't forgive him.

Activity

Was Angela wrong? Write a different ending that shows Angela following Jesus' example of forgiveness.

_____

_____

_____

_____

How can we experience God's peace?

Hear & Believe

✝ Scripture   The Unforgiving Servant

Peter asked Jesus, "Lord, if my friend sins against me, how often must I forgive him? Seven times?"

"Not seven times, but seventy-seven times," Jesus said. "God's kingdom is like a king who lent his servant a large sum of money. When the king asked for his money back, the servant begged for more time to pay. Feeling sorry for his servant, the king forgave him and said that he didn't owe him anything."

"Later, the servant saw a man who owed him a little money. The servant demanded to be paid. The other man pleaded for more time, but the servant had him put in prison. When the king heard this, he was angry. 'You wicked servant! I forgave you that large debt. You should have forgiven the small one! You are going to jail,' the king said." Then Jesus said, "My children, your heavenly Father wants you to forgive everyone from your heart."

Based on Matthew 18:21–35

Prayer and Forgiveness

Jesus instructs Peter about forgiveness by telling a **parable** story. In the story, the king represents God who is ready to forgive debts that were so great that they could never be repaid. Instead of learning the lesson about forgiveness, the servant condemns to prison another man who owes him a small amount of money.

In teaching us the Lord's Prayer, Jesus calls attention to this lesson on forgiveness with the words, "Forgive us our trespasses as we forgive those who trespass against us." The prayer reminds us that, just as God is ready to forgive us, we are called to forgive even the greatest wrongs.

Our Church Teaches

The Seventh through Tenth Commandments tell us to avoid being selfish. When we are unwilling to forgive, it is a sign of our selfishness. This is the same selfishness that leads people to want what is not theirs. It is the same selfishness that leads people to tell lies to avoid their responsibilities to others. Jesus teaches us to be as generous as God our Father. We are to share all the wonderful gifts God has given us, including his **peace** and forgiveness.

Faith Words

parable
A parable is a story that teaches a moral or religious lesson. Parables use everyday events and objects to explain important truths.

peace
Peace follows forgiveness. It is the calm, good feeling of being together with others and with God.

How can Scripture show us how to forgive?

Respond

 ## Living the Seventh Through Tenth Commandments

The Seventh through Tenth Commandments require us to give proper respect and care for the rights of others. Everyone has the right to the things he or she needs to live. We should not be envious of things that belong to others. We should respect our families and the families of others. If we fail, we must do what we can to make up for our actions and ask for forgiveness.

Activities

1. The chart below lists the Seventh, Eighth, Ninth, and Tenth Commandments. In the space next to each Commandment, write a sentence or two about what you think it means and how you can obey it.

The Ten Commandments	What this Commandment means to me and how I can obey it
VII You shall not steal.	
VIII You shall not bear false witness against your neighbor.	
IX You shall not covet your neighbor's wife.	
X You shall not covet anything that belongs to your neighbor.	

2. Look up the following Scripture passage in the Bible. Then, in your own words, write what God is telling us about forgiveness.

Luke 15:8–10

_____

_____

_____

_____

GO TO page 19 to review how to look up a Scripture passage.

186

3. Learn to sign the following phrases from the Lord's Prayer. Review what you learned in Chapters 4, 8, and 12.

| Give | us | this | day |

| our daily | bread; | and forgive | us our |

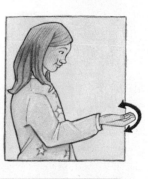

| trespasses | as we | forgive | those who |

| trespass | against | us. |

How does God want me to forgive others?

Prayer Celebration

A Prayer for Peace

Reader: A reading from the letter of Paul to the Colossians.

Holy and beloved, God has chosen you as his special people.

Be compassionate, kind, humble, and gentle. Be patient with one another and forgive anyone who has hurt you. If one person is upset with another, forgive as the Lord has forgiven you.

Over all these things, put on love. It ties everything together perfectly. Each one of you is part of the Body of Christ. Let the peace of Christ guide your hearts.

Reader: The word of the Lord.

All: Thanks be to God.

Based on Colossians 3:12–16

Leader: Pause and think about the above reading. Complete the following sentences that speak of forgiveness.

It is sometimes hard for me to forgive someone when

_____

_____.

A quality that I could use to help me forgive others is

_____

Leader: Together, let us pray the Lord's Prayer by using sign language.

All: Our Father. . .

A Complete the sentences with names from the box.

~~Jesus~~	Peter
~~unforgiving servant~~	~~king~~

1. I did not show mercy toward a man who owed me money.

<u>Unforgiving servant</u>

2. I said that you should forgive your neighbor seventy-seven

times. <u>Jesus</u>

3. I asked Jesus how often I must forgive my friend if he sinned

against me. <u>Peter</u>

4. I forgave my servant and said he didn't owe me anything. <u>King</u>

B Respond to the following.

1. Explain what a parable is. <u>a story that teaches</u>
<u>the moral or religion lesson.</u>
_____
_____
_____

2. Explain how obeying the Seventh through Tenth Commandments
helps us in our relationship with others.

<u>Helps us avoid being selfish</u>
_____
_____
_____

The Ministry of Lector Lectors proclaim the Word of God at Mass, usually the First Reading and Second Reading during the Liturgy of the Word. If the Responsorial Psalm is not sung, they might also read the psalm and lead the people in the response. A priest or deacon reads the Gospel. To do the best job possible, lectors prepare by prayerfully reading the Scriptures they will proclaim. And they make sure they can pronounce correctly any difficult names of people or places.

In Everyday Life

Activity Fill in the blanks and take turns making each announcement with expression.

1. Ladies and gentlemen, please welcome _____!

2. Let's all join in wishing _____ the best birthday ever!

3. Please join us after school today to support the best soccer team in

   _____!

In Your Parish

Activity Look back at the Scripture reading on page 188. Underline the words you do not understand the meaning of. Circle the words you are not sure how to pronounce. Then write one sentence to summarize the reading. Share your results with a partner.

Summary: _____

_____

_____

_____

_____

Social Justice

Jesus taught that the way to holiness is to serve others. Today the Church is dedicated to serving the poor and disadvantaged throughout the world.

As I have done, so you must do.
Based on John 13:15

The Last Supper probably took place upstairs in a house such as this. The painting from a twelfth century manuscript shows Jesus washing the feet of a disciple at the supper.

Song of the Body of Christ/ Cancíon del Cuerpo de Cristo

Words by David Haas
Spanish translation by Donna Peña

NO KE AND'AH AHI, Hawaiian traditional
Arranged by David Haas

REFRAIN

We — come — to share our sto-ry, we — come to break the bread, — We — come — to know our ris - ing from the dead.
Ve - ni-mos a de-cir del mis - te-rio, y par - tir el pan de vi-da. Ve - ni-mos a sa-ber de nuew - tra e - ter - ni - dad.

VERSE

1. We — come — as your peo - ple, we — come — as your own, u - nit - ed with each oth - er, love — finds a home.
2. We are called to heal the bro - ken, to be come — as your own, we are called to feed the hun - gry at our door.
3. Bread of life and cup of prom - ise, in this meal we all are one. In our dy - ing and our ris - ing, may your king - dom dome.
4. You will lead and we shall fol - low, you will be the breath of life; liv - ing wa - ter, we are thirst - ing for — your light.
5. We will live and sing: "A - lo - ha," "Al - le - lu - ia" is our song. May we live in love and peace our whole life long.
   (live and sing your prais - es,)

D.C.

© 1989, GIA Publications, Inc.

Take Home

FAMILY TIME

Our Vocation to the World

At Baptism we become a sign of God's love for the world. Jesus said, "This is how all will know that you are my disciples, if you have love for one another" (John 13:35). The work we do should reflect our vocation of Christian love.

ACTIVITY

Who Am I? Describe the qualities of an occupation. Tell what the person does and what he or she needs to do his or her job. See if others in your family can guess who that person is!

WEEKLY PLANNER

On Sunday
As a family, identify the different ministries people take part in at Mass. Don't forget the assembly!

On the Web
www.blestarewe.com

Visit our Web site for the saint of the day and the reflection question of the week.

Saint of the Week

Saint Louis IX
(1214–1270)

Saint Louis IX of France became king of France at age twelve and married seven years later. He had eleven children. Louis, a man of great integrity, was religious, just, respectful of all people, trustworthy, and a man of peace.

Patron Saint of: Archdiocese of St. Louis, Missouri; parenthood
Feast Day: August 25

A Prayer for the Week

Help us today, God, to search for goodness and, like Saint Louis, do everything we can to make your world better. Give us the wisdom to see how we can best do your work. Amen.

Take Home

FAMILY TIME

✚ Scripture Background

In the Time of Jesus

Lamps   A simple oil lamp was the main source of light in a Palestinian home. Originally made of clay, it was decorated with geometric or floral designs. A basic lamp had at least one wick and burned constantly, possibly to help light other household fires when needed. Olive oil was usually used as fuel since it gave off less smoke than fat. Typically, the lamp was kept on a wooden or ceramic lampstand.

In Matthew 5:14–16, Jesus uses the image of a lamp on a stand to show how we are to be a light to the world.

OUR CATHOLIC TRADITION in Art

Pietro Perugino   Jesus called Saint Peter to be the head of the Church. On the side walls of the Sistine Chapel in the Vatican, one painting stands out above all the rest. It is *Christ Giving the Keys to St. Peter* (1482) by Pietro Perugino.

Perugino was one of the greatest fresco, or wall, artists of the time. In this painting the descending diagonal running from Christ to the kneeling Peter immediately draws the eye to the central event. Perugino's more famous pupil, Raphael, painted frescoes in the Vatican as well, but not in the Sistine Chapel.

CONTVRBATIO·IESV·CHRISTI·LEGISLATORIS

17 Our Vocation to the World

LET US PRAY Let your light shine before all.

Based on Matthew 5:16

◇ ◇ ◇

Share

God calls all Catholics to do the work of the Church. We continue Christ's mission in the world by serving those who are in need. Our light is Christ living in us. It shines as we share God's love with others.

Activity

Read the headlines about ways people do Christ's work. Then write your own headlines about a person or group you know who serves others.

> ### Children Sign Up for Walkathon to Help Poor

> ### Rescue Teams Sent to Help Earthquake Victims

>

> ### Neighbors Help Rebuild House After Fire

>

How do we show others the goodness of God?

Hear & Believe

✝ Scripture The Light of the World

*In Jesus' time there were no electric lights, so nights were
very dark. An oil lamp was the only light in a house. It was
placed on a stand so that everyone would be able to see.
Jesus told his followers that they were to be the light of
the world. They were to be an example to help all see
the goodness of God. Jesus called himself the Light of
the world. He calls each of us to be like him.*

Jesus said, "You are the light of the world.
You are like a city on a mountain. Everyone
can easily see you. People do not put their
lamp under a basket. Instead they put
it on a stand for everyone to see. Like
that lamp, your light must shine
for others. People will see
your good deeds and glorify
your heavenly Father."

Based on Matthew 5:14–16

Serving Others

As Christians, we are called to use our special talents to serve those in our community and the world. The type of work we do to serve God and others is called a **vocation**. Some people carry on Christ's mission as members of a religious community. Men who are called to serve God as priests, deacons, or bishops celebrate the Sacrament of **Holy Orders**. Every person who is baptized has a vocation to serve God and other people.

All vocations are important. Each of us has different talents, but we share in the work of Christ.

 page 274 to read more about vocations.

Priest, Prophet, and King

Through Baptism and Confirmation, we join all Christians in bringing peace and justice to the world. Like Jesus we are anointed as priest, prophet, and king. When people ask us to pray for them or if we do a kind act for someone, we are fulfilling our role as priest. As a prophet we spread God's message of goodness and love to others. Leading and serving others with justice and mercy helps us to live out our role as king.

Our Church Teaches

In Holy Orders, men are chosen for the special ministry of the priesthood. God wants each of us to serve others. Through our vocations, we help people to understand his kingdom. God will judge us on how well we love our neighbor, especially those who are poor or suffering.

To help us in our vocation, we pray in union with the **Communion of Saints**. We ask the followers of Jesus, including those who have died, to help us to live God's message of peace and love.

We Believe

We share Christ's role as Priest, Prophet, and King with those who are baptized. Through our vocations we carry on Christ's mission in the world.

Faith Words

vocation
A vocation is the work we do as members of the Church. We are called to use our talents to carry on Christ's mission in the world.

Communion of Saints
All people living and dead who believe in Jesus Christ make up the Communion of Saints.

How do people use their individual talents to do the work of Christ?

Respond

Saint Louis IX Let His Light Shine

King Louis IX of France is a light for us to follow. Throughout his life, Louis praised God, fulfilling his baptismal role as priest. He also served God as the husband of Margaret and the father of eleven children. In 1235, Louis followed his vocation to be the ruler of France.

He shared in Christ's role as prophet when he spread God's message of peace and justice to the people of France. He was well-known for his fairness and honest treatment of the people under his rule.

King Louis IX shared in Christ's role as king when he served all the people of France, especially those in need. He reached out to the poor and established hospitals for the sick. He also worked to provide a good education for his people.

We admire King Louis IX because he ruled with justice and helped bring God's peace to the people of France. We celebrate the feast day of Saint Louis IX, King of France, on August 25.

Following Others

We can talk to adults for help in understanding what our vocation may be. We can join adults who are doing God's work. This will help us learn about the many ways we can serve God and others.

Activities

1. Look at the pictures. Discuss how each person is being a light to others.

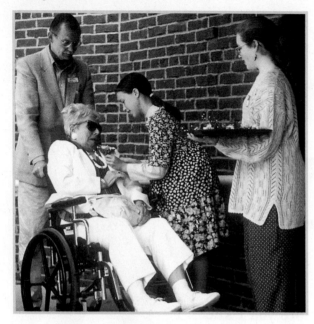 

2. Write about how you might like to serve others when you are older.

_____

_____

_____

_____

_____

_____

_____

3. Rearrange the four words to write a sentence that tells what all Christians should do.

    others   love   with   serve

_____

How does
Jesus help us
serve others?

Prayer Celebration

Prayer Before a Crucifix

Look at the picture of the crucifix as you pray this prayer together.

All: O good and gentle Jesus, before you I kneel. I pray that you will deepen my faith, hope, and love in you. I ask you to help me follow in your ways. I see your five wounds and think about how you suffered. I love you for your great sacrifice and promise to share your love with others.

Based on Indulgence Prayer Before a Crucifix

Leader: How can you share Christ's role as Priest, Prophet, and King? Let us quietly think about our vocation.

(As the leader reads the following prayer, follow the directions after each phrase.)

Leader: Lord Jesus Christ, *(Everyone breathes in.)*

Son of God, *(Everyone breathes out.)*

protect me *(Everyone breathes in.)*

and guide me. *(Everyone breathes out.)*

A **Circle** the letter of the best answer.

1. All people living and dead who believe in Jesus Christ make up the _____
   a. Church
   b. prophets
   c. religious community
   d. Communion of Saints

2. The work we do as members of the Church is called our _____
   a. vocation
   b. devotion
   c. prayer
   d. job

3. Men called to serve God as priests, deacons, or bishops celebrate the Sacrament of _____
   a. Penance and Reconciliation
   b. Baptism
   c. Holy Orders
   d. Confirmation

4. Through Baptism, Jesus anoints us as priest, _____, and king.
   a. friend
   b. Apostle
   c. prophet
   d. angel

5. In the "Prayer Before a Crucifix", we think of Jesus' _____ wounds and how he suffered for us.
   a. five
   b. four
   c. three
   d. two

B **Respond** to the following.

1. What did Jesus mean when he told his followers to be the light of the world? _____

_____

2. Write about how a person you know uses his or her talents to light the world. _____

_____

Faith in Action

Ministries to the Unemployed In many parishes, there are people who have lost their jobs and are unable to find work. Like families, parish communities support and encourage its members in difficult times. The unemployed have many different needs that the parish can help meet. A parish can help provide food and money as a family tries to get back on its feet. We can bring people together to talk about the many ways unemployment affects their lives. We can bring people together who can help one another find jobs. And we can help know that brighter days lie ahead.

In Everyday Life

Activity Think of some jobs people do for us that we tend to take for granted. Think how much harder our life would be without them.

List three of these jobs here.

1. _____

2. _____

3. _____

In Your Parish

Activity The phrase *in the same boat* means that a group of people are in a similar situation. They understand one another and can help one another. Choose one or more of the words below to use in a sentence that describes one way people who are "in the same boat" of unemployment can help one another. Then pray for the unemployed of your parish.

pray	babysit	share	invite	respect
talent	write	hug	newspaper	meet

_____

_____

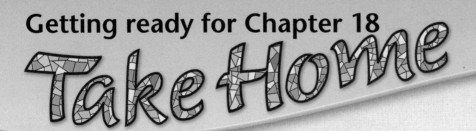

The Eucharist

The bread of life is the gift Christ left us when he died. How to make it central to our life is the challenge that faces all Catholics. We often think that we must be self-reliant, but God invites us to come to the Eucharist for help.

ACTIVITY

Grains of Wheat   What are the ingredients needed to make bread? Look in a recipe book to see. Talk with your child about how important each ingredient is for the recipe to work properly. Relate this to how each person is important in making up the Body of Christ.

WEEKLY PLANNER

On Sunday

Remind your child that the Eucharist is kept in the tabernacle. The candle, or sanctuary lamp, reminds us that Christ is present.

On the Web

www.blestarewe.com

Visit our Web site for the saint of the day and the reflection question of the week.

Saint of the Week

Saint Alphonsus Liguori (1696–1787)

Saint Alphonsus Liguori was a bishop and doctor of the Church. Alphonsus began a career as a lawyer, and later decided to become a missionary. He organized a group of priest missionaries, now known as the Redemptorists.

Patron Saint of: vocations
Feast Day: August 1

A Prayer for the Week

Your Body gives us life, dear Lord. Keep us strong and faithful like Saint Alphonsus Ligouri. May we never tire of your care for us. Amen.

Take Home

FAMILY TIME

✠ Scripture Background

In the Time of Jesus

Bread   Every morning women worked for hours to make bread for their families. They began by using a hand mill to grind the kernels of barley or wheat into flour. After mixing it with other ingredients, the women shaped the dough into round thin disks, about seven inches in diameter. They baked the bread on hot stones or in ovens located outside the home. Typically, a person ate three loaves of bread at every meal. Besides being a staple food, bread is also associated with religious rites.

Read about the bread Jesus shared with his disciples in Mark 14:12–16; 22–26.

OUR CATHOLIC TRADITION in Church Teachings

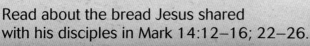

The Year of the Eucharist   In what turned out to be the final year of his pontificate, Blessed Pope John Paul II proclaimed 2005 as the Year of the Eucharist. In his encyclical on the Eucharist, the Holy Father wrote, "The Church draws her life from the Eucharist. This truth does not simply express a daily experience of faith, but recapitulates the heart of the mystery of the Church" *(Ecclesia de Eucharista, 1)*. In October 2005, as this special year came to a close, newly elected Pope Benedict XVI was asked by a child how Jesus

Christ can be truly present in the Eucharist. He said, "We do not see him with our eyes, but we see that wherever Jesus is, people change—they improve… We do not see the Lord himself, but we see the effects of the Lord: so we can understand that Jesus is present."

18 The Eucharist

. . . through their merits and prayers, grant that in all things we may be defended by your protecting help.

Eucharistic Prayer I

Share

The people we love help us learn about God and the world around us. Even when they are not with us, we think of them when we do certain things. What they teach is a part of us.

Activity

Role-Play

Choose who will play the following roles and act out the story.

Narrator: The Salerno family gathered in the park for a special reunion. Everyone was there except Grandpa. He had died a few months earlier.

David: "I miss Grandpa. I sure wish he was here to help us catch a fish."

James: "He always knew just when to pull in the line."

Narrator: The two boys stood by the edge of the lake and cast their lines. Suddenly David noticed something different about James's line.

David: "Reel it in!"

Narrator: James pulled in his line and was surprised to see a large fish dangling from the hook.

James: "That's just like Grandpa always did it! It feels like he is here with us."

How do we become one in Christ?

Hear & Believe

 ## Worship Gathered as One in Christ

On Sunday, God's family gathers at Mass to celebrate the Eucharist. The Eucharist unites us with God and the Church. The Church includes all those living on Earth and all those who have died as followers of Christ. Like Mary and all the saints, we are together in Christ. During the celebration of the Eucharist, the **assembly** honors the saints by praying the following prayer.

> In communion with those whose memory we venerate, especially the glorious ever-Virgin Mary, Mother of our God and Lord, Jesus Christ, and blessed Joseph, her Spouse, your blessed Apostles and Martyrs . . . and all your Saints; we ask that through their merits and prayers, in all things we may be defended by your protecting help.
>
> *Eucharistic Prayer I*

The Eucharist

The Eucharist is the center of Catholic life and the memorial of Christ's Passover. We express our faith in Jesus, who died on the Cross for our sins, and joyfully celebrate his Resurrection. Through his Son, Jesus, God shows us his kingdom of justice, mercy, and love.

The Eucharist unites us to all members of the Church.

The Role of the Priest

In the name of Christ, the priest celebrates the Eucharist with the assembly at Mass. He leads the assembly in the celebration of the sacrifice of our Salvation—the life, Death, and Resurrection of Jesus Christ. The priest brings Jesus' message of love each time he proclaims the **Gospel** and preaches the **homily**.

At Mass the priest leads the assembly in prayer. He asks the Holy Spirit to make Christ present for us. Through the Holy Spirit, the gifts of bread and wine are changed into the Body and Blood of Christ.

The priest also presides over the other Sacraments with the Catholic community. He guides members of a parish in their journey of faith. United with the priest through the Eucharist, together we help bring God's love and mercy to the world.

Our Church Teaches

The priest has the important role of leading the Church in the liturgy. At Mass we celebrate the Eucharist with the Communion of Saints. Christ brings all Christians together—those who are living and those who have died. Each time we celebrate the Eucharist, we grow stronger in our faith. In the Eucharist we are united with God and with one another.

We Believe

The Eucharist is central to our Catholic faith. We remember how Jesus freed us from sin by his Death and Resurrection.

Faith Words

assembly
Catholics gathered to celebrate the Eucharist and other Sacraments are called the assembly.

Gospel
The Gospel is a reading from the New Testament about the life and teachings of Jesus Christ.

Papal Mass, Central Park, New York, 1995

How can we describe the Eucharist?

Respond

When we receive the Eucharist, we realize that we are one Body of Christ.

Activities

1. Draw a box around the words or phrases that refer to the celebration of the Eucharist. In the blank boxes, write your own words or phrases that describe the Eucharist. Use the word bank below to help you.

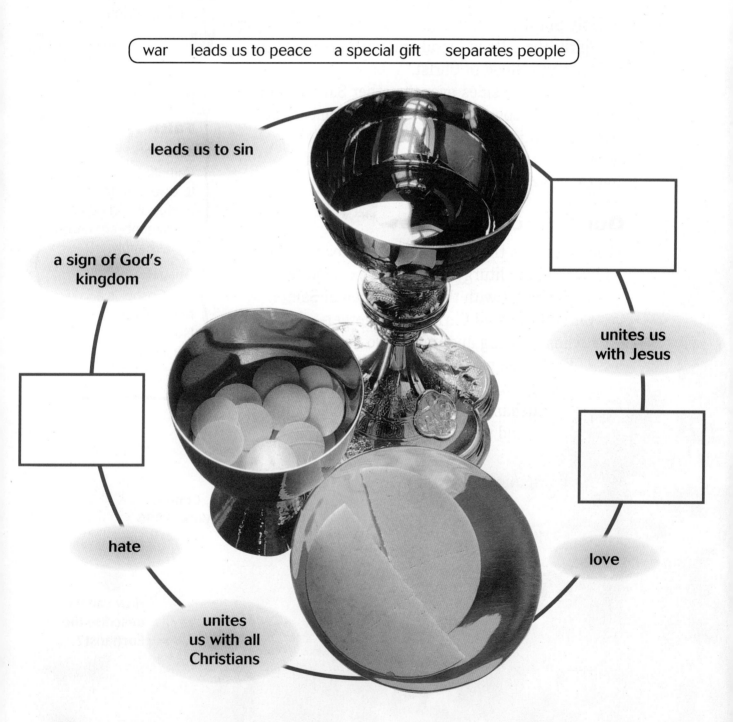

war   leads us to peace   a special gift   separates people

leads us to sin

a sign of God's kingdom

unites us with Jesus

hate

love

unites us with all Christians

2. The priest has a special vocation to lead the Catholic community in prayer. Draw a picture of a priest celebrating a sacrament. Below your picture, write how the priest leads members of the Catholic community in that Sacrament.

GO TO pages 262–265 to review the Seven Sacraments.

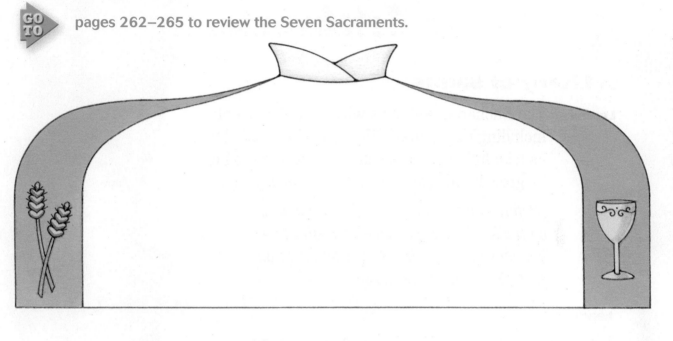

_____

_____

_____

_____

3. In addition to celebrating the liturgy, the priest ministers within the parish. Think about a priest you know and then complete the sentence.

Father _____ helps people in the parish by

_____

_____

_____

_____

How can we ask the saints to pray for us?

✠ Prayer Celebration

A Litany of Saints

Leader: The Eucharist unites us with all God's people, including the saints in Heaven. The saints lived as true followers of Jesus. We ask them to help us grow in faith and love as we follow Jesus.

(Before you begin praying the litany, write on the line below the name of a saint that you know and admire. As the leader prays each line, pray the response.)

Leader:	**All:**
Lord, have mercy	Lord, have mercy
Christ, have mercy	Christ, have mercy
Lord, have mercy	Lord, have mercy
Holy Mary, Mother of God	pray for us
Saint Joseph	pray for us
Saint Monica	pray for us
Saint Augustine	pray for us
Saint Francis	pray for us
Saint Clare	pray for us
Saint John Vianney	pray for us
Saint Teresa	pray for us
_____,	pray for us
All holy men and women	pray for us
Lord, be merciful	Lord, save your people
From every sin	Lord, save your people
By your death and rising to new life	Lord, save your people
Lord Jesus, hear our prayer	Lord Jesus, hear our prayer

Based on the Litany of Saints from the Rite of Baptism

A **Match** column A with column B by writing the correct number in the space provided.

A

1. Litany of Saints

2. assembly

3. Gospel

4. homily

5. Eucharist

6. priest

B

_2_ Catholics gathered to celebrate the Sacraments

_4_ special talk the priest gives after reading the Gospel

_6_ guides members of the parish in their journey of faith

_1_ special prayer to the saints

_5_ unites us with God and one another

_3_ a section of the New Testament about the life and teachings of Jesus Christ

B **Circle** the hidden words and complete the sentences about the Eucharist.

1. We celebrate the Eucharist at _mass_.

2. The Eucharist _unites_ us with God and the Church.

3. The Eucharist is the memorial of Christ's _passover_.

4. When we celebrate the Eucharist, we grow stronger in our _faith_.

```
P M T Q A M U N
G A H M A S S O
P A S B P K U F
I L S S J N N S
Q F A N O T I R
W A V M U V T N
Z F A I T H E U
D E L V C X S R
```

Faith in Action

Extraordinary Ministers of Holy Communion   Extraordinary ministers of Holy Communion help the parish priest meet the needs of all the people who wish to receive Holy Communion. After special training, they bring the Sacrament to people who are sick at home, in nursing homes, and hospitals. To emphasize that these volunteers bring with them the love and prayers of the parish community, the celebrant at each parish Mass often gives a special blessing to the people who will visit the sick during the coming week.

In Everyday Life

Activity   On the line below, write the name of someone you feel especially close to. Then draw two images that would help others understand why you feel this way about the person you named.

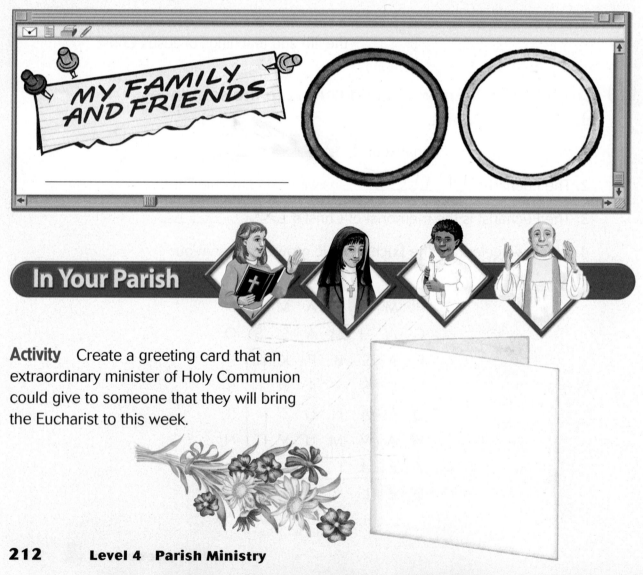

MY FAMILY AND FRIENDS

In Your Parish

Activity   Create a greeting card that an extraordinary minister of Holy Communion could give to someone that they will bring the Eucharist to this week.

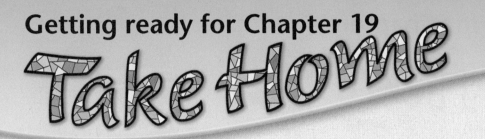

The New Commandment and the Works of Mercy

There are people who are so afraid of breaking rules that they can become paralyzed when they have to make a decision. Jesus often challenged the rules that governed civil and religious practice. He had respect for the law but taught that the law was made for people, not the other way around. The law Christ teaches is simple but demanding. It requires us to use love as the standard by which we judge our actions.

ACTIVITY

Loose Change   Make a donation box and put it in a special place. One day this week, ask your whole family to collect loose change and place it in the box. Take the money collected and give it to a charity, such as Catholic Relief Services or your parish.

WEEKLY PLANNER

On Sunday

Look in your parish bulletin for ways people offer service to the community. Is there something that your family could participate in?

On the Web

www.blestarewe.com

Visit our Web site for the saint of the day and the reflection question of the week.

Saint of the Week

Saint Louise de Marillac (1591–1660)

Saint Louise de Marillac founded the Daughters of Charity community in 1633. She was a friend of Saint Vincent de Paul, who depended on her assistance. She was an intelligent and generous woman and had great stamina and determination.

Patron Saint of: social workers
Feast Day: March 15

A Prayer for the Week

Lord, help us to be good stewards of all the good things you have given us. As we remember the good works and deeds of Saint Louise, give us the strength to spread your love. Amen.

Take Home

FAMILY TIME

✠ Scripture Background

In the Time of Jesus

Beggars   In New Testament times, beggars were commonly seen outside the temple gates or along the roads. Making up about fifteen percent of the population, they were forced to live outside the cities and villages. With little or no support from their families, they begged for food or alms. Beggars were often blind or suffered from other disabilities or illnesses. Jesus embraced the begging poor and taught his followers to treat them with compassion.

In Matthew 25:31–41 Jesus invites us to ease the sufferings of others by caring for their physical needs.

OUR CATHOLIC TRADITION in Film

Monsieur Vincent   In 1948 a popular film was made about Saint Vincent de Paul, called *Monsieur Vincent*. It tells the story about the sixteenth-century saint growing up in a poor family. He was a bright, charming, ambitious boy who was drawn to the priesthood. He became wealthy and was even chaplain to the queen. Then in midlife he discovered his vocation to serve the poor. He devoted his talents to serving the underprivileged, especially prisoners and slaves, and used his association with the rich to fund his charitable projects. He founded the Vincentian Order of priests and helped Saint Louise de Marillac to establish the Sisters of Charity.

Pierre Fresnay as Saint Vincent de Paul in *Monsieur Vincent*

19 The New Commandment and the Works of Mercy

This is my commandment:
love one another as I love you.

John 15:12

Share

Jesus knew the needs of others. He asks us to follow his example and help spread God's love to the world. We can love others in simple ways every day.

Activity

In the blank hearts, use words or pictures to show how you share God's love with others.

Listen to someone with a problem

smile

What does Jesus promise for those who follow the Law of Love?

Hear & Believe

✝ Scripture Seeing Christ in Others

In Chapter 11 we learned that at the Last Supper, Jesus gave his disciples a New Commandment to love one another. When we follow this Law of Love, we see Christ in others and treat them with kindness and mercy. How do we see Christ in others? Read what Jesus says.

"When the Son of Man returns in glory with angels all around him, he will sit on a glorious throne. Everyone will gather before him, and he will separate them, like a shepherd separates his sheep from goats.

"He will place the sheep on his right and the goats on his left. Then he will say to those on his right, 'Come, you are blessed by my Father and shall inherit the Kingdom of God. You are blessed because when I needed food and drink, you nourished me. When I needed a friend, you welcomed me. When I needed something to wear, you gave me clothes. When I was sick and needed attention, you cared for me. When I needed a friend in prison, you visited me.'

"Then the blessed will ask, 'When did we give you food and drink? When did we welcome you? When did we give you clothes? We don't remember seeing you sick or visiting you in prison. When did we do these things?'

"The Son of God will reply, 'Whenever you helped someone in need, you helped me.'"

Based on Matthew 25:31–41

Called to Serve

Jesus combined the Ten Commandments and the Beatitudes into one Law of Love known as the New Commandment. We can follow this Law of Love by doing daily acts of kindness. By treating others as God would want, we can love as Christ loves.

GO TO page 273 to read more about the New Commandment.

The Corporal Works of Mercy

The loving acts described in this chapter from Matthew 25:31–41 are called the **Corporal Works of Mercy**. The Corporal Works of Mercy tell us how to respond to the basic physical needs of all people. Jesus asks us to love others as he loves us.

The Corporal Works of Mercy

Feed the hungry.

Give drink to the thirsty.

Give clothing to the poor.

Visit those in prison.

Shelter the homeless.

Visit the sick.

Bury the dead.

The Spiritual Works of Mercy

Jesus also wants us to listen and respond to people as they express their thoughts and emotions. He asks us to reach out lovingly to people who are lonely, discouraged, or struggling in life. Jesus wants us to pray for their needs. To encourage and support others in these ways, we use the **Spiritual Works of Mercy** as our guide.

Spiritual Works of Mercy

Help others do what is right.

Teach the ignorant.

Give advice to the doubtful.

Comfort those who suffer.

Be patient with others.

Forgive injuries.

Pray for the living and the dead.

Our Church Teaches

Jesus said that we should love others as he loves us. Jesus showed God's love to others by taking care of their basic needs. The Corporal Works of Mercy are ways we can care for the physical needs of others. The Spiritual Works of Mercy show us ways to encourage, guide, and give emotional support to others.

Faith Words

Corporal Works of Mercy

The Corporal Works of Mercy are the loving actions by which we respond to the basic physical needs of people.

Spiritual Works of Mercy

The Spiritual Works of Mercy are the loving actions by which we respond to the basic spiritual needs of people.

How can we take care of the basic needs of others?

Dr. Albert Schweitzer and Caring for Others

Albert Schweitzer was born in Germany in 1875. He was aware of the needs of others even as a child. One way Albert learned about caring for others was by reading the Bible.

At school he noticed that some of the children were poorly dressed or had less food than he did. Albert was uncomfortable with this difference.

When he got older, he enrolled in medical school and become a doctor. On a trip to Africa, Alfred saw people who were poor and sick. He decided to help those who were suffering there. He and his wife, Helene became famous for practicing the Corporal Works of Mercy. They built a hospital at Lambarene in Africa. There they took care of the sick, and shared all they had with others.

Albert won the 1952 Nobel Peace Prize for the care he gave to the sick people in Africa. Dr. Albert Schweitzer died in 1965 and is buried at Lambarene.

Activity

Begin at **Start** on the game board. Roll one dice and move the correct number of spaces following the direction of the arrows. If you land on a picture, tell which Work of Mercy is being shown. If you land on the name of a Work of Mercy, give an example of someone doing this Work of Mercy. It can be someone at school, in your family, in your community, or in the world.

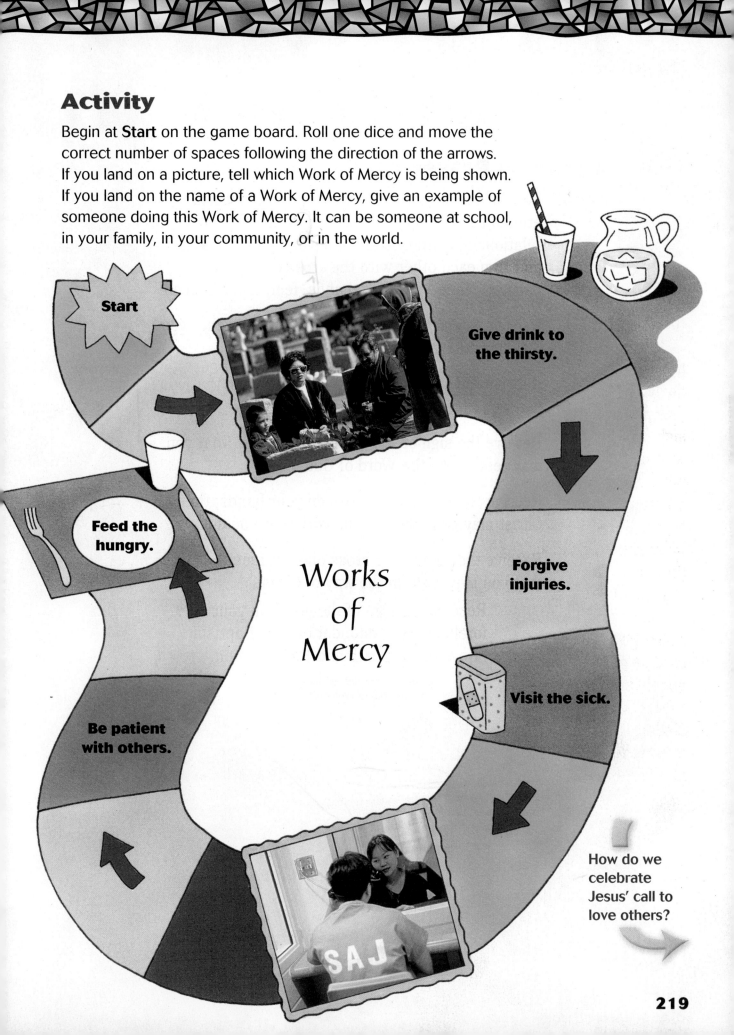

Start

Give drink to the thirsty.

Feed the hungry.

Works of Mercy

Forgive injuries.

Visit the sick.

Be patient with others.

How do we celebrate Jesus' call to love others?

✝ Prayer Celebration

A Signing Prayer

Leader: Each of our senses helps us relate to the world around us. The senses also help us in our relationship with God and his people. Let us bless and sign each other with the cross over your partner's ears, eyes, lips, hands, feet, and forehead.

Receive the sign of the cross on your ears, that you may hear the voice of the Lord.

Receive the sign of the cross on your eyes, that you may see the glory of God.

Receive the sign of the cross on your lips, that you may respond to the Word of God.

Receive the sign of the cross on your hands, that Christ may be known in the work that you do.

Receive the sign of the cross on your feet, that you may walk in the way of Christ.

Receive the sign of the cross on your forehead as a reminder of your Baptism into Christ's Death and Resurrection.

Based on the Rite of Acceptance and Rite of Welcoming, RCIA

19 Chapter Review

A **Write** the letter "C" for a Corporal Work of Mercy or "S" for a Spiritual Work of Mercy.

1. __C__ Visit those in prison.

2. __S__ Comfort those who suffer.

3. __S__ Be patient with others.

4. __C__ Shelter the homeless.

5. __S__ Help others do what is right.

6. __C__ Visit the sick.

7. __C__ Give drink to the thirsty.

8. __S__ Teach the ignorant.

9. __C__ Bury the dead.

10. __S__ Forgive injuries.

11. __S__ Pray for the living and the dead.

12. __C__ Give clothing to the poor.

13. __C__ Feed the hungry.

14. __S__ Give advice to the doubtful.

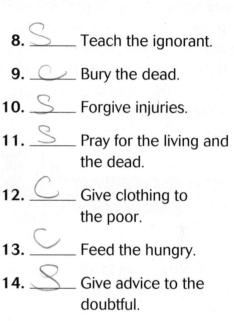

B **Respond** to the following questions.

1. How did Dr. Albert Schweitzer share God's love with others?

_____

_____

_____

2. How can you follow the Law of Love? _____

_____

_____

_____

3. When have you shared what you have with others?

_____

_____

_____

Faith in Action

Ministries to the Poor While some poor people live on the streets of our nation's biggest cities, some live in the house or apartment right next to our own. Others are barely surviving on their farms. Many volunteer organizations in the United States and throughout the world welcome poor people seeking shelter, food, and clothing. Volunteers also reach out to find people in need who may be too afraid or embarrassed to ask for help. And they work with local communities and governments to try to improve the conditions that cause poverty. The Corporal and Spiritual Works of Mercy taught by Jesus inspire their work.

In Everyday Life

Activity Write an article for your local newspaper suggesting some of your ideas on ways to help the poor in your community.

_____

_____

_____

_____

In Your Parish

Activity Write or draw one way people in your parish can take care of the spiritual needs of others.

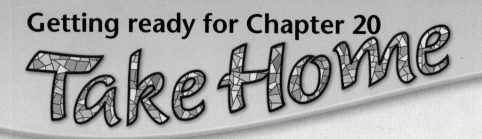

FAMILY TIME

The Commandments and Bringing God's Message to the World

No matter how closely a parent watches a child, he or she cannot be present all the time to protect or guide in difficult situations. Catholic parents know that God's assistance is available through prayer.

ACTIVITY

Prayer Table Locate a place in your home where your family can pray this week. If you have a favorite prayer card or statue, consider displaying it there. In addition to religious articles, you can place a family picture at your prayer table. Each person in the family can put a prayer request on the table as well.

WEEKLY PLANNER

On Sunday

Before the Sign of Peace at Mass, listen to the words of Jesus regarding peace and unity.

On the Web

www.blestarewe.com

Visit our Web site for the saint of the day and the reflection question of the week.

Saint of the Week

Blessed Junípero Serra (1713–1784)

Blessed Junípero Serra was a Spanish Franciscan priest who built nine of the 21 missions in California and traveled extensively throughout the state. The international Catholic organization the Serra Club is named after Blessed Junípero. This organization is dedicated to the promotion of vocations to the priesthood and religious life.

Feast Day: July 1

A Prayer for the Week

Lord, Junípero Serra brought the Gospel and education to the Native Americans of California. Help us to follow you in our own lives and to always know your peace. Amen.

Take Home

FAMILY TIME

✝ Scripture Background

In the Time of Jesus

Galilee   Most of Jesus' ministry was centered in Galilee, the northern section of Palestine. It was fertile land with olives, grapes, and wheat growing throughout the countryside. A main feature of the region was the Sea of Galilee where fisherman could be seen casting their nets. Just west of the lake is the village of Cana where Jesus performed his first miracle. While attending a wedding there, Jesus changed water into wine. After his Resurrection, Jesus returned to Galilee with a special message for his disciples.

Read about the commissioning of the disciples in Matthew 28:16–20.

OUR CATHOLIC TRADITION in Art

The Angelus   The Angelus is a prayer that people have prayed since the Middle Ages. The prayer consists of the dialogue between Mary and the angel Gabriel, interspersed with a series of Hail Marys, followed by a closing prayer. By the fourteenth century, church bells were tolled at six in the morning, noontime, and six in the evening, reminding people to pray the prayer. The painting *L'Angélus* by Jean-Francois Millet (1814–1875) shows that wherever people are, they pause to pray this special prayer. This devotion is still popular today in many churches.

L'Angélus, (1857–1859) by Jean-Francois Millet

20 The Commandments and Bringing God's Message to the World

Go and make disciples of all nations.

Based on Matthew 28:19

Share

Through prayer we can grow as Christians. We can pray for God's help as we try to bring God's peace and justice to the world.

Activity

Complete the prayer below. You may use the words that are listed or your own ideas.

| sad | sick | poor | fighting |

I see people who are lonely;

  help me extend my hand in friendship.

I see people who are suffering;

  help me ease their pain.

I see people who are _____;

  help me _____.

I see people who are _____;

  help me _____.

Lord, forgive me when I fail to do something I should for people.

How do we bring peace and justice to the world?

Hear & Believe

✝ Scripture The Commissioning of the Disciples

After Jesus' Resurrection, he came to the disciples in Galilee. He told them what God wanted them to do, saying: "Go and travel to all nations. Teach the people there what I have commanded. Baptize them in the name of the Father, the Son, and the Holy Spirit. You also will show them how to become disciples of mine. And remember, I will always be with you."

Based on Matthew 28:16–20

The Power of Prayer

God is always with us, especially when we pray. He touches our hearts with his love and strengthens us to live his law of love.

As Catholics, we have a responsibility to show God's goodness to one another. Prayer helps us feel the power of God's love and then share it with others. Through prayer, we listen to God's call to do what is good. We can ask God to help us do better.

Prayer helps us work against the sin and evil in the world. We can pray a prayer of **petition** to ask for God's forgiveness when we fail to do his will. We can also ask for God's help in bringing his love to the world.

When we need God's help to live as he asks, we can pray, "Dear God, help me to love others as you love me."

 GO TO page 275 to read more about prayer. Go to pages 15 and 16 to pray the Rosary and the Stations of the Cross.

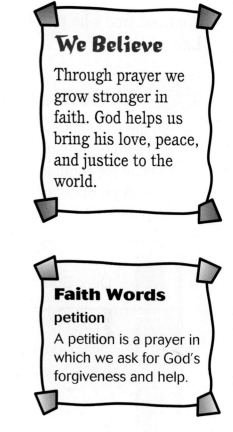

We Believe

Through prayer we grow stronger in faith. God helps us bring his love, peace, and justice to the world.

Faith Words

petition
A petition is a prayer in which we ask for God's forgiveness and help.

Our Church Teaches

As Christians, we are called to bring God's love, peace, and justice to the world. We lift our hearts in prayer, asking for God's help to ease the suffering of others. Our prayers of petition are heard by God, who is always with us. Through prayer, following the Ten Commandments, and living the Law of Love, we help to bring God's love, peace, and justice to the world.

How does prayer help us grow in understanding our faith?

Respond

We need God's help to follow the Commandments and live the Law of Love.

 **Activities**

1. On the lines below, write a prayer of petition for both the Fourth and Fifth Commandments. Then select and write a prayer of petition for another Commandment. Commandments one and two have been done for you. Refer to the Ten Commandments chart on page 272 for help.

I	Dear God, help me to keep you first in my life.
II	Dear God, help me to always use your name respectfully.
IV	Dear God, _____ _____ _____
V	Dear God, _____ _____ _____ _____
	Dear God, _____ _____ _____

We Must Love Everyone

2. Write ways that you can bring peace and justice to others.

_____

_____

_____

_____

_____

We Must Love Everyone

3. Learn to sign the following phrases from the Lord's Prayer.
Review what you learned in Chapters 4, 8, 12, and 16.
You can now sign all of the Lord's Prayer!

And lead

us not into

temptation,

but deliver

us

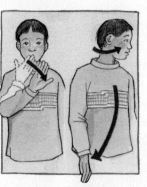
from evil.

Amen.

How do we pray for justice and peace?

✝ Prayer Celebration

A Commitment Prayer

Leader: In our world today, be an instrument of peace. Where you find hateful words, be acceptance and love. Where you find prejudice and ignorance, be a source of knowledge and truth. Where you find fear and doubt, be a sign of faith and confidence. Where you find darkness and poverty, be committed to the basic dignity of every person. Where you find violence, be compassion and peace. You are children of the light; be a sign of the living Gospel!

All: Amen.

Based on the Prayer of Saint Francis, adapted by the Capuchin Youth and Family Ministries Center, Garrison, NY

Leader: Together, let us pray the Lord's Prayer, using sign language.

All: Our Father . . .

20 Chapter Review

A Complete the sentences with words from the box.

peace	petition	grace
love	pray	goodness

1. When we pray, God touches our hearts with

   his __love__.

2. A __petition__ is a prayer in which we ask
   for God's forgiveness and help.

3. God is always with us, especially when we __pray__.

4. Following the Commandments and the Law of Love, we bring

   God's love, __peace__, and justice to the world.

5. As Catholics, we have a responsibility to show

   God's __goodness__ to one another.

B Circle the letter of the best answer.

1. The commitment prayer from
   page 230, is based on a prayer
   of Saint ___.
   a. Joseph
   b. Martin de Porres
   c. Francis of Assisi
   d. Patrick

2. Jesus told his disciples
   to ___ what he had commanded.
   a. remember
   b. explain
   c. remind people of
   d. teach others

3. Jesus promised his disciples
   that he would ___.
   a. think about them often
   b. always be with them
   c. perform many miracles
   d. build a church for them

4. Prayer helps us work against
   sin and ___ in the world.
   a. evil
   b. justice
   c. sacrifice
   d. helplessness

Faith in Action

The Rosary Altar Society   Some people say that prayer is like the air we breathe. We don't always see or hear it, but it is so important that without it, we could not live. Our prayers, as well as the actions we take as a result of our prayers, can make a big difference. The Rosary Altar Society, serving in many parishes, started more than a hundred years ago as a group devoted primarily to praying all the mysteries of the Rosary together every week. Today, their ministry often includes such tasks as caring for altar linens, vestments, and candles and making baptismal garments.

In Everyday Life

Activity   Interview a friend to find out what he or she thinks is one of the most important ways that the world we live in needs to change. Ask what your friend wants people to pray for to help the situation. Take your interview notes below.

Something that needs to change: _____

_____

How prayer can help: _____

_____

In Your Parish

Activity   Prayer and action go hand in hand. Use your own words to write a prayer to help support one or more of the social ministries that people in your parish are actively involved in.

My prayer for the ministry of _____

_____

_____

_____

FEASTS AND SEASONS

The Liturgical Year   **234**

Blessed Teresa of Calcutta   **237**

Saint Martin de Porres   **239**

Our Lady of the
Miraculous Medal   **241**

Advent   **243**

Christmas   **245**

Lent: Remembering
the Cross   **247**

Lent: A Prayer Celebration   **249**

Three Holy Days   **251**

Easter   **253**

Pentecost Sunday   **255**

The Assumption of
the Blessed Virgin Mary   **257**

The Liturgical Year

The Church year is called the liturgical year. During the liturgical year, we celebrate special seasons and feasts that help us remember important times in the life of Jesus. We also celebrate special feasts that honor the Blessed Virgin Mary and the saints.

Holy Week begins on Passion Sunday. It ends with the three holiest days of the Church year. We call these three days "the Triduum."

HOLY WEEK

HOLY WEEK

The Church year begins with the **Advent** season. For four weeks, we prepare for the birth of Jesus. We count the four weeks by lighting the candles on the Advent wreath.

ADVENT

ADVENT

The liturgical year begins.

The **Triduum** begins on Holy Thursday evening and ends on Easter Sunday evening. During these three days, we remember the Last Supper, Jesus' Death on the Cross to save us from sin, and his Resurrection from the dead.

During the **Easter** season, we celebrate the Resurrection of our Lord Jesus Christ. This season lasts for fifty days. It is time of great joy.

EASTER

The season of **Lent** begins on Ash Wednesday and lasts for forty days. During Lent, we prepare for Easter, which is the greatest feast of the Church year. We get ready for Easter by praying and doing good acts.

The season of **Ordinary Time** has two parts. The first part is between Christmas and Lent. The second part is between Easter and Advent. During Ordinary Time, we learn about the life and teachings of Jesus.

LENT   **ORDINARY TIME**

The **Christmas** season begins with the Solemnity of the Nativity (Christmas). On Christmas Day, we celebrate the birth of Jesus. We thank God our Father for sending his only Son to be our Savior.

CHRISTMAS

The Liturgical Year

The Church guides us in celebrating the great events and people of our faith through the seasons and feasts of the liturgical year. The special feasts of the liturgical year include Sundays and the holy days of obligation.

Sunday

Sunday is the Lord's Day. On Sunday, we celebrate the Resurrection of our Lord Jesus Christ. Sunday is so important that the Church requires us to attend Mass. We gather with our family and parish community to give thanks to God for sending his Son to save us.

Holy Days of Obligation

The holy days of obligation are six special days when we honor Jesus, the Blessed Virgin Mary, and the saints. Like Sundays, these holy days are so important that the Church requires us to attend Mass. In the United States, the Church celebrates the following holy days of obligation.

The Immaculate Conception of the Blessed Virgin Mary December 8	We celebrate that Mary, the Mother of Jesus, was conceived without Original Sin.
The Nativity of the Lord (Christmas Day) December 25	We celebrate the birth of Jesus, our Savior.
Mary, the Holy Mother of God January 1	We celebrate that Mary is the mother of God's Son, Jesus Christ.
The Ascension of the Lord forty days after Easter Sunday (or the Seventh Sunday of Easter)	We celebrate the moment when Jesus, in his resurrected body, returned to his Father in Heaven.
The Assumption of the Blessed Virgin Mary August 15	We celebrate that Mary was taken body and soul into the glory of Heaven. She fully shares in the Resurrection of Jesus.
All Saints November 1	We celebrate all the people who lived holy lives on Earth and who now live with God in Heaven.

Blessed Teresa of Calcutta

Together, we can do something beautiful for God.

Blessed Teresa of Calcutta

People We Admire

Most of us are fortunate enough to know at least one person whom we admire. The word *admire* means "to have a high regard for." This person may be courageous, kind, or patient. We look at this person and try to be more like him or her.

Activity

Imagine that you are giving an award to someone you admire. Name the person and describe why you admire him or her.

Award of Admiration

Merit

Serving the Poorest of the Poor

Agnes Gonxha Bojaxhiu (boi yah jee oo) was born in Yugoslavia in 1910 to parents who were from Albania. Along with many of her friends, Agnes belonged to a Catholic group for young girls that was dedicated to Mary.

While she was still a teenager, Agnes knew that God was calling her to serve him in a special way. She eventually joined an Irish order of religious sisters and volunteered to do mission work in India. Agnes took the name Teresa as her religious name and taught high school in Calcutta. Sister Teresa loved her life as a sister and as a teacher. But soon Sister Teresa felt that God was calling her to do more.

Sister Teresa decided to start an order of sisters of her own. These sisters would do the hardest work of all—they would care for those who were very poor and had no one to care for them. Sister Teresa became known as Mother Teresa. Soon her order grew to several thousand women from India and around the world who wanted to serve the poorest of the poor. The sisters also cared for children who had no families, were very ill, or had been neglected. The sisters loved all these people with the same love as Jesus.

In 1997, Mother Teresa died, but her order, the Missionaries of Charity, continues her important work throughout the world. The Feast of Blessed Teresa of Calcutta is celebrated on September 5.

Blessed Teresa of Calcutta, we believe that you are with God in Heaven. Pray for us that we may see Jesus in the poor as you did, and love him and care for him in serving them. Amen.

Saint Martin de Porres

Turn from evil, and do good.

Based on Psalm 34:15

Teasing Diana

It is almost time for the bell to ring. Diana hopes her mom will be waiting outside the school for her. Diana doesn't like taking the school bus because some of the kids on the bus tease her. Sometimes they tease her about her backpack. Other times they make fun of her clothes or the way she's wearing her hair that day. It is the worst time of the school day for Diana.

The bell rings. Mr. Patterson dismisses the students from his homeroom. Diana is the first student out the door. Her mother isn't waiting for her today. Slowly Diana turns toward the school bus.

Activity

Imagine that you are riding on Diana's school bus. How will you act toward her? What will you do or say?

_____

_____

_____

_____

_____

_____

A Saint of Compassion

Martin de Porres was born in Lima, Peru in 1579. Martin was not accepted in his town because he was a child of a man from Spain and a black woman freed from slavery. People made fun of him. They teased him. They called him names.

When Martin was a teenager, he became an assistant to a man who was a pharmacist, doctor, and surgeon. Martin soon learned to help others with the skills he learned. He wanted to do more for people who were hurting, so he decided to join the Dominicans. The Dominicans are an order of priests and brothers who work with the poor, the sick, and those who need schooling. Martin asked if they would take him in as a helper. But the priests and brothers soon recognized that Martin was a holy man who had many gifts to offer their order and the poor of Peru. They asked Martin to be a lay brother. Martin eagerly agreed. This opportunity was more than he had ever hoped for.

Martin spent much of his time tending to the sick and injured. He worked with the poor and spent many nights praying and fasting.

Because Martin suffered from the cruelty of others, he could see when people were sad. Martin spent his life caring for those who were hurting, with compassion and love.

The Feast of Saint Martin de Porres is celebrated on November 3.

Saint Martin de Porres, we can learn from you what it means to be gentle and kind to all people. Pray with us for those who are hurting this day. Amen.

Our Lady of the Miraculous Medal

✝ O Mary, conceived without sin, pray for us.

Based on the Prayer to Our Lady of the Miraculous Medal

Why Catholics Wear Medals

The Miraculous Medal is one of the most common medals that Catholics wear. But there are others. Most have images of saints on them. Why do Catholics wear medals? To remind us of the holy people, such as Mary and the saints, who can help us and pray for us. When we think of Mary and other holy people, we are reminded what it means to lead good lives.

Activity

Design your own religious medal. Draw a picture or write a prayer in the space provided. Then write a sentence about why you chose this image or prayer. Share your medal and response with a partner.

A Reminder of Mary's Love and Protection

The Blessed Virgin Mary is the Mother of Jesus, our Savior. She is our Mother, too. Sometimes, God sends Mary to give us a message. We call these special visits from Mary *apparitions* or visions. In 1831, God sent Mary to give a special message to a young French nun. Here is the story of Mary's visit to the young woman.

At the age of 24, Zoe Labouré joined the Daughters of Charity and took the name Catherine. Several months later, Sister Catherine began to have visions of the Blessed Virgin Mary. In one vision, an angel woke Sister Catherine and led her to the convent chapel. There she saw Mary sitting in a chair by the altar. They quietly spoke together for more than two hours. In the next and most famous vision, Sister Catherine saw an image of the Miraculous Medal. This medal has the image of Mary on one side. Around the image are the words *"O Mary, conceived without sin, pray for us who have recourse to thee."* On the other side of the medal is the letter *M* with a cross above it. Below the *M* are images of the hearts of Jesus and Mary.

Mary told Sister Catherine to have many medals like this made. She said that whoever wore the medal would receive great graces from God. Sister Catherine told a priest about her visions. The priest believed Sister Catherine and went to see the archbishop. The archbishop gave his permission to have the medals made.

Many Catholics throughout the world wear the Miraculous Medal. The Miraculous Medal reminds us of how much God and Mary love us and protect us. We celebrate the Feast of the Miraculous Medal on November 27. On November 28, we celebrate the Feast of Saint Catherine Labouré.

> Saint Catherine Labouré, Mary asked you to do something great for her by giving the world her Miraculous Medal. Thank you for giving us a way to remember Mary and all that she did for us for Jesus' sake. Amen.

Advent

Look! There is the Lamb of God, who has come to take away our sins.

Based on John 1:29

Who Are You, Mike?

My name is Adam and I'm in fourth grade. I live in Illinois with my mom and my three sisters. My brother, Mike, is married and lives with his wife and their new baby in the next town.

I thought I knew my brother pretty well when he lived with us at home. Mike is everything to me. He is a dad, a big brother, and my best friend.

When Mike joined the Navy, I was always hoping for a letter from him. When I did receive a letter, I would read it slowly and carefully because it showed me another side of my brother that I didn't know anything about. This Mike was so intelligent and wise, so full of life, and very funny!

When I watch Mike care for his son, Andrew, I see yet another side of Mike. He is gentle and loving, caring and tender. Mike is probably the proudest dad in the world.

Just when you think you know someone, he or she can surprise you. Mike sure did surprise me—and he still does!

Activity

Adam's story shows us how we can come to know someone in different ways. Tell about the different ways you have come to know someone.

_____

_____

_____

_____

The Three Comings of Jesus

Advent is the time the Church uses to help us prepare to meet Jesus in three ways. We know that on Christmas we remember and celebrate Jesus' coming in Bethlehem more than 2,000 years ago. We call this coming into our lives Jesus' coming in *history*.

Jesus continues to come to us each day. He no longer comes as a baby born to Mary and Joseph. Jesus' coming into our lives each day is called *mystery* because it cannot be completely understood. We can meet Jesus in our families, in our friends, or in other people who show that they care about us. We can recognize him when we see those who are poor, hurting, ill, or without hope.

Before Jesus returned to his Father in Heaven, he promised to return to Earth as our King. We call that coming of Jesus at the end of time *majesty*. On that day, Jesus will reign over God's kingdom on Earth. God's kingdom will be a kingdom of peace and justice, abundance and joy.

Advent gives us four weeks to prepare to remember, celebrate, and look forward to Jesus' comings in history, mystery, and majesty.

Jesus, come to us each day. Help us prepare to welcome you as our King in the fullness of God's kingdom. Help us to recognize you in one another. Amen.

Christmas

 The Word of God became human and made his home among us.

Based on John 1:14

The Coming of Jesus

Christmas Day and the entire Christmas season is a time of great joy in our Church. It is a time to remember, believe, and celebrate.

Activity

In each ornament, write one thing you remember, believe, and celebrate about Jesus.

I remember my family putting the Christmas lights and decorating my house and my Christmas tree

I believe in Jesus and virgin Mary

I celebrate Jesus's birth on December 25th

Christmas: A Time to Remember, Believe, and Celebrate

Christmas is a time to remember. We remember that God kept his promise to send a Savior. We remember that God loved us so much that he sent his own Son to be that Savior! And we remember that Jesus is the Light of the world when we use Christmas candles, lights on our Christmas trees, window lights, and luminaries.

Christmas is a time to believe. We believe that Jesus is God's Son and the Second Person of the Holy Trinity. We believe that he was born, lived among us, and died on a cross. And we believe that he rose again and shares new life with us.

Christmas is a time to celebrate all that we remember and believe about Jesus. At Mass, our parish community sings of his birth, prays to him at the crèche, and hears about this special child in Scripture. Here is a tiny infant who needs Mary, his mother, and Joseph, his foster father, to care for him. Yet the angel calls this helpless child the Son of the Most High, the shepherds praise God for his birth, and the Magi travel from the East to honor him. Through the Eucharistic celebration, the community unites in joy. We thank and praise God for sending us Jesus, the Savior of the world.

Jesus,
help us always to remember your great love for us. We believe that you are the one sent to us by God. Be with us in all our Christmas celebrations.
Amen.

Lent: Remembering the Cross

✝ Jesus was led away, and, carrying a heavy cross, went to the place where he was to be crucified.

Based on John 19:16–17

Remember Me

The Jenkins family and the Arturo family lived next door to each other for several years. When Mr. Arturo received a big promotion at his company, he and his family had to move across the country to Denver, Colorado.

"It just won't be the same in this neighborhood now," Kelly said to her best friend, Ramona.

Ramona couldn't imagine not having Kelly right next door to her. But Ramona tried to make Kelly feel better. "I'll never forget you, Kelly. We'll be friends for life!"

Activity

List some things Kelly and Ramona can do to stay in touch and remember each other.

_____

_____

_____

_____

_____

_____

_____

_____

The Stations of the Cross

Our Church wants to remember always the great sacrifice that Jesus made for us through his suffering and Death on a cross. One way our Church remembers Jesus' love for us is by recalling his journey to Calvary. Calvary is the hill where Jesus died. We call this special devotion the Stations of the Cross or the Way of the Cross. Sometimes Christians visit the Holy Land, Israel, and actually walk the same path as Jesus. Usually we recall the journey by reflecting and praying at each Station.

There is no one way to pray this traditional Lenten devotion. Sometimes the priest, deacon, or lay minister leads the group from Station to Station inside the parish church, or outside on the parish grounds. At each Station, we recall what took place at that Station in Jesus' journey to Calvary. Next we pause briefly and allow time for silent prayer and then sing a hymn about Jesus' journey to Calvary.

Often an extra Station of the Cross is added to the first fourteen. This Fifteenth Station tells our belief that Jesus' story didn't end with his Death on a cross. The Fifteenth Station tells us that Jesus rose from the dead. We remember with joy that Jesus' sacrifice ended in new life for him and for all his followers.

GO TO page 16 to read more about the Stations of the Cross.

> Jesus, through your suffering, Death, and Resurrection, you won new life for us. Help us always to remember your great love for all people. Amen.

Lent: A Prayer Celebration

✝ Lord, we are your people. Hear us whenever we call upon you. You have made us your own and set us free.

A Prayer for Renewal

Activity

Jesus' friends help one another to follow him. Pick one of the situations below and think of a saying or words of advice that you might give someone facing this problem. Then on an index card or a separate sheet of paper, use markers to write and decorate these words of wisdom to share with a member of your class.

___ You don't want to do your homework or your chores.

___ Someone is making fun of you.

___ You feel lonely.

___ It is hard to be patient and kind.

Leader: Blessed be God, the giver of Salvation. Lord, you commanded that human beings should be given new life.

All: Lord, renew us.

Leader: Lord, you promised us a new Heaven and a new Earth. Renew us every day through your Spirit so that we may be with you forever in Heaven.

All: Lord, renew us.

Leader: Help us to work with you to bring justice, love, and peace to everyone.

All: Lord, renew us.

Leader: Free us from being careless and lazy. Give us the gift of your grace.

All: Lord, renew us.

Leader: Deliver us from evil. Keep us from being blind to goodness.

All: Lord, renew us.

Reader: Pray for one another that you might find healing. If someone is slipping away from truth and goodness, help him or her. Remember this: The person who helps another avoid evil will save his or her own soul.

Based on James 5:16, 19–20

All: Father, help us to understand the meaning of your Son's Death and Resurrection. Teach us to remember it in our lives every day. Grant this through our Lord Jesus Christ, your Son, who lives and reigns with you and the Holy Spirit, one God, forever and ever. Amen.

Based on the Liturgy of the Hours, First Week of Lent

Three Holy Days

Joseph of Arimathea took Jesus' body down from the Cross, wrapped him in a burial cloth, and laid him in a tomb.

Based on Luke 23:53

The Triduum

The three days between Holy Thursday and Easter Sunday are the most important time of celebration in the Catholic Church. These three days are called the Triduum (TRIH doo uhm). This is a Latin word that means "three days."

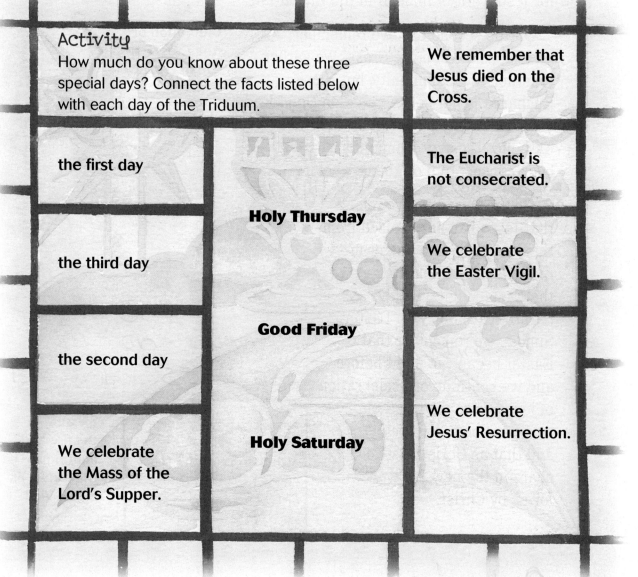

Activity
How much do you know about these three special days? Connect the facts listed below with each day of the Triduum.

We remember that Jesus died on the Cross.

the first day

The Eucharist is not consecrated.

Holy Thursday

the third day

We celebrate the Easter Vigil.

Good Friday

the second day

We celebrate Jesus' Resurrection.

Holy Saturday

We celebrate the Mass of the Lord's Supper.

Celebrating the Triduum

The Triduum has been celebrated for centuries, since the days of the early Church. These three days celebrate Jesus' Passion, Death, and Resurrection.

The first day of the Triduum begins on the evening of Holy Thursday. This is because in ancient times the beginning of the day was when the sun set, not dawn or midnight. So the first day begins with our celebration of the Mass of the Lord's Supper. We recall and give thanks for Jesus' gift of himself in the Eucharist.

Washing of feet on Holy Thursday

On the second day, we remember how Jesus died on the Cross. We gather together as a community, but the Eucharist is not consecrated on Good Friday. This is the only day in the year when Catholics receive Communion that has been consecrated on the day before.

Adoration of the Cross on Good Friday

On the third day, we rejoice that Jesus has been raised from the dead and is no longer in the tomb. We celebrate the Easter Vigil on Holy Saturday evening. On Easter Sunday we remember that Easter began the night before and we continue our celebration of joy. We are glad that our sins have been forgiven and that as Christians we share in the new life won for us by Christ.

Jesus, you gave up your life for us on the Cross. Now you are at the right hand of God, our Father. Remember us, lead us, and care for us. Amen.

Blessing of the fire and lighting of the candle at Easter Vigil

Easter

Why do you look for him among the dead? He is alive!

Based on Luke 24:5–6

A Reason to Celebrate

It was mid-February. The weather had turned very cold and icy. Alicia worked an extra shift at the hospital that night because some of the relief nurses couldn't make it into work. She was very tired when she started for home.

When Alicia was halfway home, her car slid off the road and was stuck in a ditch. All bundled up, Alicia tried to keep warm. She hoped help would come soon, but the night had never seemed so scary or long.

Five hours later, a state police officer spotted Alicia's car in the ditch. He helped Alicia into his patrol car, put the heat on high, and gave her a cup of hot coffee from his thermos. Alicia was so grateful.

After a tow truck came and towed Alicia's car out of the ditch, Alicia drove the rest of the way home. When her husband, Ted, saw her pulling into the driveway, he rushed outside to meet her. Ted hurried Alicia into the house, and together they shared a hot breakfast. They had the best reason of all to celebrate—Alicia was safe after a very dangerous time.

Activity

Think about the best reason you ever had to celebrate. Describe it here.

_____

_____

_____

The Church's Greatest Celebration

It is time to put away our sadness. It is time for celebrations of joy and new life. Easter has come!

We know that something wonderful has happened when we walk into our parish church on Easter Sunday. The colors are bright and beautiful. The songs are happy and filled with praise. We have new water for blessing and baptizing and a new fire to remind us of Jesus, the Light of the world. The Paschal candle is new and will remind us of Easter joy as it is lit each Sunday. It will also be lit at each Baptism that is celebrated, bringing the new life of Jesus to each new Christian.

At Mass on Easter Sunday, we are sprinkled with the water that was blessed the night before at the Easter Vigil. The blest water reminds us that we are each a new creation—our old lives have passed away and we are new in Christ, our Savior. We use again the Church's word of praise and thanks—*Alleluia*! We pray and sing, "Alleluia! Jesus is risen! We will live forever!"

Risen Jesus,
come into our hearts this Easter season. You are the reason we celebrate all the blessings in our lives, especially the gift of new life we received at Baptism.
Amen.

Pentecost Sunday

LORD, send out your Spirit, and renew the face of the Earth.

Based on Psalm 104:30

Everyone Needs a Helper

When you were a very young child, you needed help with almost everything. Now that you are older, you can do many more things on your own. When you become an adult, you will be able to do even more things without anyone else's help. But even adults sometimes need a helper.

Activity

Complete the activity by filling in the blanks.

When I was a baby, I could do these things by myself.

_____

_____

_____

_____

Now that I am older, I can do these things alone.

_____

_____

_____

I still need a helper to …

_____

_____

_____

The Coming of the Holy Spirit

When the Jewish feast of Pentecost came, the followers of Jesus were in Jerusalem. They had locked themselves in an upstairs room out of fear.

Suddenly, there came a noise like a strong wind blowing. What appeared to be tongues of fire rested on each person's head. All were filled with the Holy Spirit. The disciples were no longer afraid. The Helper promised to them by God had come. They began to speak of Jesus and his teachings with great courage to all who had come to Jerusalem for the feast.

Based on the Acts of the Apostles 2:1–11

The Holy Spirit Is Our Helper

On Pentecost, we celebrate the coming of the Holy Spirit, the Spirit of God. The Scripture passage above tells us that the Spirit of God was sent to the early Church on the Jewish feast of Pentecost. It was on this day that God fulfilled his promise to send a helper. The Holy Spirit would help Jesus' friends remember all that he had taught them. The Holy Spirit would help them live their lives in imitation of Jesus, the Lord.

In our Church today, we sometimes call the Solemnity of Pentecost Sunday the birthday of the Church because on that first Pentecost, the Church community was born. The disciples began to teach and preach with great courage about Jesus of Nazareth and all that took place through his Death and Resurrection.

> Spirit of hope, help us always to be a Church committed to following the Gospel of Christ in doing the Father's will. Amen.

Pentecost

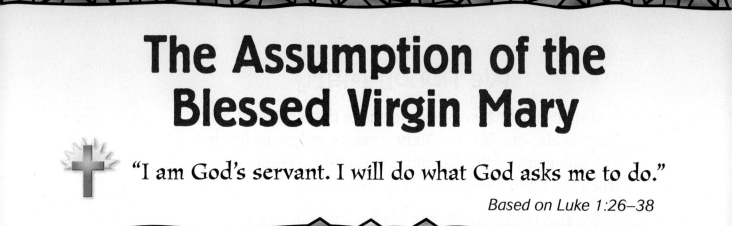

The Assumption of the Blessed Virgin Mary

"I am God's servant. I will do what God asks me to do."

Based on Luke 1:26–38

Mary, the Mother of God

Mary is important because she is the Mother of God. She is a good example for us because she chose to obey God. Catholics have always remembered Mary's special role in our Church.

Activity

One of the ways we remember Mary is through the use of symbols. Using the three symbols of Mary as examples, create your own symbol. Then color all four to create a banner honoring Mary.

the sun and moon, from a vision of Mary in the Book of Revelation

tear drops, for the sadness Mary experienced

a lily, which means purity

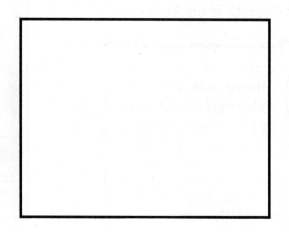

We Honor Mary

Catholics honor Mary because she is the Mother of Jesus. Mary is also our Mother. Mary loves us and cares for us. The Solemnity of the Assumption is an important day when the Church celebrates the life of Mary.

We also remember Mary's life because she is a great role model. She obeyed God perfectly. We read in the Bible how God sent the angel Gabriel to ask Mary if she would be Jesus' mother. Mary had a choice. She could have said no. Instead, Mary chose to do God's will. Mary said, "I am God's servant. I will do what God asks me to do."

Based on Luke 1:26–38

Mary Is Taken to Heaven

Mary kept her promise to God. She stayed with Jesus until his Death on the Cross. We do not know how long Mary lived. Our Church believes that Mary was taken up into Heaven to be with God. Her body and spirit are there. This is called the Assumption, and we celebrate it on August 15.

> Mary, you are now in Heaven with Jesus. You understand what it means to be scared, sad, brave, and prayerful. Please watch over us and ask God to bless us. Amen.

OUR CATHOLIC HERITAGE

What Catholics Believe

About Revelation 260

About the Trinity 260

About the Catholic Church 261

About Mary and the Saints 261

How Catholics Worship

About the Sacraments 262

About the Sacraments
of Initiation 262

About the Sacraments
of Healing 264

About the Sacraments
at the Service of Communion 265

About the Mass 266

About Reconciliation 269

How Catholics Live

About Conscience 270

About Faith, Hope, and Love 270

About the Beatitudes 271

About the Commandments 272

About Vocations 274

How Catholics Pray

About Prayer 275

About Kinds of Prayer 275

About the Lord's Prayer 276

WHAT CATHOLICS BELIEVE

We believe in all that our Church teaches.

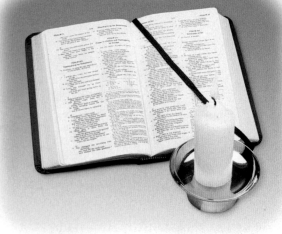

ABOUT
REVELATION

God speaks to us through Sacred Tradition
and Sacred Scripture.

Sacred Tradition

Sacred Tradition includes the Church's official teachings and customs
that have been handed down by the Apostles over the centuries.

Sacred Scripture

Sacred Scripture, or the Bible, is the written Word of God. We believe
that the Holy Spirit inspired the writers of the Bible. Sacred Scripture
is made up of the Old Testament and the New Testament.

ABOUT
THE TRINITY

We believe that there is One God in Three Divine Persons. We call the
mystery of One God in Three Divine Persons the Holy Trinity. The Three
Persons are the Father, the Son, and the Holy Spirit.

God, Our Father

God, the First Person of the Holy Trinity is the Creator of all life and
he is our Father. It is Jesus, God's only Son, who taught us to call God
"Father." Through our Baptism, God became our Father and we became
his children. Jesus told us that our Father in Heaven loves us always.

Jesus Christ

Jesus Christ is the Son of God. By the power of the Holy Spirit, Jesus
was born of the Blessed Virgin Mary. He suffered and died on the Cross
to save us from sin and death.

The Holy Spirit

After he returned to his Father in Heaven, Jesus sent the Holy Spirit to
his disciples. The Holy Spirit will guide the Church until the end of time.
We receive the Holy Spirit at Baptism and in the other Sacraments.

ABOUT

THE CATHOLIC CHURCH

We believe in one, holy, catholic, and apostolic Church.

The Church is one. We believe in one God. We believe in one faith and in one Baptism. We believe that the Catholic Church is one because we are joined together when we believe in Jesus Christ.

The Catholic Church is holy because Jesus Christ, with the Father and the Holy Spirit, is holy. It is by God's grace that we are holy.

The Church is catholic, or universal, because we welcome all people as Jesus does.

The Church is apostolic. Apostolic means that the Church is founded on the teachings of Jesus Christ and the Apostles. We believe the chief teacher of the Church is the pope. When he speaks for the Church about faith or morals, we believe that the pope represents Jesus on Earth.

ABOUT

MARY AND THE SAINTS

Mary, the Mother of Jesus, is our greatest saint. Mary was filled with grace from the first moment of her life. She lived a life without sin. Mary loved and cared for Jesus, and she loves and cares for us. Catholics honor Mary as the Mother of Jesus and the Mother of the Church.

We believe that we are joined with all those who believe in Jesus Christ. We believe that the lives of the saints show us how to live as Jesus taught us. We honor the saints and ask them to pray for us. We believe that one day we will live with all the saints forever with God.

The Black Madonna

HOW CATHOLICS WORSHIP

We celebrate our faith in worship when we give honor and praise to God. Worship is so important to the Catholic community that the Church calls it the first "work" of God's people.

ABOUT

THE SACRAMENTS

As Catholics, we gather in community to worship when we celebrate the Seven Sacraments. The Sacraments are the **sacred** signs that celebrate God's love for us. The Sacraments join us with Jesus Christ. Each Sacrament has special words and actions. Through these words and actions, God becomes present to us in the church community.

The Sacraments are divided into three groups to help us understand their words and actions. The first group is called the Sacraments of Initiation.

ABOUT

THE SACRAMENTS OF INITIATION

We become full members of the Catholic Church through the Sacraments of Baptism, Confirmation, and Eucharist.

Baptism

Baptism is the Sacrament of welcome into the Church. When we are baptized, we receive the Holy Spirit. We are anointed and marked with the sign of the cross. We begin our journey of faith and begin to grow in holiness.

At Baptism the priest or deacon prays, "I baptize you in the name of the Father, and of the Son, and of the Holy Spirit" (Rite of Baptism).

The priest or deacon pours water over the head of the person being baptized or immerses the person in the water. This is a sign that we are one with Jesus Christ, through his life, Death, and Resurrection.

Confirmation

Confirmation is the Sacrament that helps us grow in holiness. In Confirmation, the Holy Spirit strengthens us in the faith and helps us share the Goods News of Jesus with others.

When we are confirmed, the bishop or priest prays, "Be sealed with the Gift of the Holy Spirit" (Rite of Confirmation).

The bishop or priest lays his hands on the head of the person being confirmed and anoints his or her forehead with oil.

Eucharist

The Eucharist is the Sacrament of Jesus Christ giving himself to us in a special way. When we worship together at Mass, we receive the Eucharist. We celebrate that Jesus Christ has given himself to us. In the Eucharist, Jesus Christ becomes present to us in the readings from Sacred Scripture. Christ becomes present in the bread and wine that have become his Body and Blood.

The priest takes the bread and says, "TAKE THIS, ALL OF YOU, AND EAT OF IT, FOR THIS IS MY BODY." He then takes the wine and says, "TAKE THIS, ALL OF YOU, AND DRINK FROM IT, FOR THIS IS THE CHALICE OF MY BLOOD" (Eucharistic Prayer).

During the Communion Rite at Mass, we receive Jesus Christ in the Eucharist.

THE SACRAMENTS OF HEALING

The Sacraments of Penance and Reconciliation and the Anointing of the Sick are called the **Sacraments of Healing.** They celebrate God's forgiveness and healing.

Penance and Reconciliation

Penance and Reconciliation, also referred to as the Sacrament of conversion, confession, or penance, is the Sacrament that celebrates God's forgiveness. God always forgives us when we are sorry. Through the sacrament, we examine our conscience, we admit our sins, we express our sorrow, and we receive absolution.

When we celebrate the Sacrament of Penance and Reconciliation, the priest prays, "I absolve you from your sins in the name of the Father, and of the Son, and of the Holy Spirit" (Rite of Penance).

The priest makes the sign of the cross as he prays this prayer of absolution.

The Anointing of the Sick

The Sacrament of the **Anointing of the Sick** celebrates God's love and healing. It is for those who are either very sick or elderly. Through the prayers of the Church and the grace of the Sacrament, people can be healed in both mind and body.

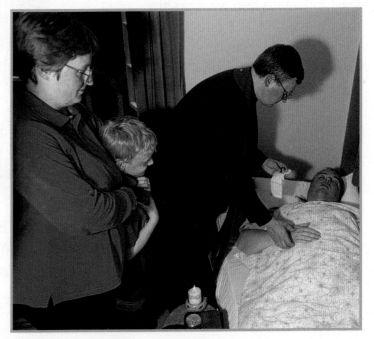

The priest prays, "Through this holy anointing may the Lord in his love and mercy help you with the grace of the Holy Spirit. May the Lord who frees you from sin save you and raise you up" (Rite of the Anointing of the Sick).

With holy oil, the priest anoints the forehead and hands of the person receiving the Sacrament of the Anointing of the Sick.

THE SACRAMENTS AT THE SERVICE OF COMMUNION

The third group of Sacraments is called the **Sacraments at the Service of Communion**. These Sacraments are Holy Orders and Matrimony. These two Sacraments celebrate two special ways that people serve God by sharing their gifts with others.

Holy Orders

Holy Orders is the Sacrament that celebrates the ordination of bishops, priests, and **deacons** to serve the Church. Bishops and priests are called to lead the Catholic community. They lead the community in celebrating the Sacraments and teaching God's Word. Deacons are also leaders in the Church. They preach homilies, preside at the celebration of some of the Sacraments, and help direct the work among the poor.

Matrimony

The Sacrament of **Matrimony** celebrates the commitment that a man and a woman make to each other. Their commitment to each other is for a lifetime. Through the grace of the Sacrament, the married man and woman are strengthened in their ability to be faithful to one another. They are called to conduct their family life as though it were a model for the whole Church.

In the celebration of the Sacrament of Matrimony, the man says to the woman, "I take you to be my wife." The woman says to the man, "I take you to be my husband" (Rite of Marriage).

In the Sacrament of Matrimony, the couple make these promises to each other in the presence of a priest or deacon and the Catholic community.

ABOUT
THE MASS

Introductory Rites

At Mass, we come together to worship God with our parish community.

Entrance Procession and Opening Hymn

As the priest and those assisting him in the Mass enter in procession, we stand and sing the opening hymn.

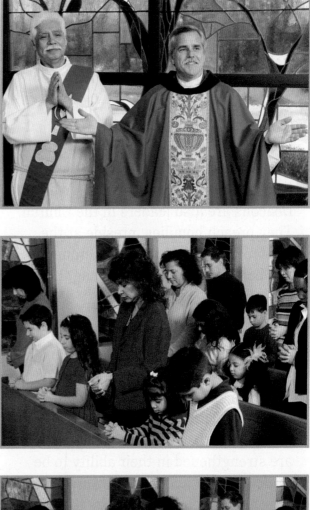

Greeting ▶

We make the Sign of the Cross. The priest welcomes us. He says, "The Lord be with you." We answer, "And with your spirit."

Penitential Act ▶

We think about our sinfulness. We ask for God's forgiveness and the prayers of the Church.

Gloria ▶

We sing the Gloria, which is a hymn of praise to God.

Collect

We pray the Collect.

Liturgy of the Word

First Reading ▶

The lector reads a story or a lesson, usually from the Old Testament.

Responsorial Psalm

We sing the response to a psalm from the Old Testament.

Second Reading

The lector reads from one of the books in the New Testament, other than the Gospels.

Gospel Acclamation

We sing "Alleluia" or another acclamation of praise as the priest or deacon prepares to read the Gospel.

Gospel ▶

We stand in reverence as the priest or deacon reads the Gospel.

Homily ▶

The priest or deacon tells us about the meaning of the Gospel and the other Scripture readings.

Profession of Faith

We recite the Nicene Creed to proclaim our belief in what the Church teaches.

Prayer of the Faithful

We pray for the Church, the pope and bishops, and for the needs of all God's people. We also pray for the needs of the members of our parish community.

Liturgy of the Eucharist

Preparation of the Altar and Gifts ▶

We bring our gifts of bread and wine to the altar. We also give gifts for the poor and donations of money for the Church.

Eucharistic Prayer

The priest begins with a prayer of praise and thanksgiving to God the Father for the wonderful gifts of creation and for the greatest gift of his Son, Jesus Christ. We sing, "Holy, Holy, Holy."

The priest recalls with us the story of the Last Supper. We hear Jesus' own words "FOR THIS IS MY BODY" and "FOR THIS IS THE CHALICE OF MY BLOOD." We sing or say, "We proclaim your Death, O Lord, and profess your Resurrection until you come again," or a similar acclamation.

At the end of the Eucharistic Prayer, we sing, "Amen."

Communion Rite

The Lord's Prayer

We pray together the prayer that Jesus taught us, the Lord's Prayer or the Our Father.

Sign of Peace

We share the Sign of Peace with those around us.

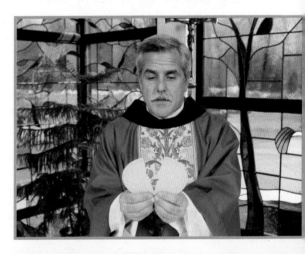

Breaking of the Bread ▶

We sing the Lamb of God as the priest and deacon prepare for the distribution of Holy Communion.

Holy Communion

We receive the Body and Blood of Christ. We say, "Amen."

Concluding Rites

Blessing

We make the Sign of the Cross as the priest blesses us.

Dismissal ▶

The priest or deacon tells us to go in peace. We sing a hymn of thanks and praise.

ABOUT
RECONCILIATION

In the Sacrament of Penance and Reconciliation, we celebrate God's forgiveness. We ask the Holy Spirit to help us better live as Jesus taught us.

Rite of Reconciliation of Individuals

Preparation

I examine my conscience by thinking of things I might have done or said on purpose that were harmful to myself or others. I remember that I may have sinned by not doing something good when I should have.

Priest's Welcome ▶

The priest welcomes me in the name of Jesus and the Church community.

Reading from Scripture

The priest may read from the Bible or may tell me a story from the Gospels.

Confession

I tell the priest my sins. The priest asks me to do a kind act or say a prayer to show that I am sorry for my sins and to remind me to be more loving.

Prayer of Sorrow ▶

I tell the priest that I am sorry for all my sins. The priest asks me to pray an act of contrition. I pray aloud the prayer of sorrow or I can make one up of my own.

Absolution ▶

Acting on behalf of the Church, the priest extends his hands over me and asks God to forgive me. The priest gives me absolution in the name of the Father, Son, and Holy Spirit.

Prayer of Praise and Dismissal

With the priest, I pray a prayer of praise. The priest tells me to go in peace. I answer, "Amen."

HOW CATHOLICS LIVE

Living as Jesus taught us is not easy, but God helps us. God gives us our conscience and three special gifts. When we turn away from sin and make good choices, we live as children of God.

ABOUT
CONSCIENCE

Our conscience is a gift from God. Our conscience helps us to know what is right and what is wrong. As Catholics, we have help in developing a good conscience. We have the Beatitudes, the Ten Commandments, and the teachings of Jesus to help us. Through the Church, the Holy Spirit guides us to understand what is right and to turn away from what is sinful.

ABOUT
FAITH, HOPE, AND LOVE

A **virtue** is a habit of doing good. Three special virtues that God gives to us at Baptism are faith, hope, and love. These virtues help us to believe in God, to trust in his promises, and to love him.

Faith helps us to believe in all that the Church teaches. It helps us to grow in truth and knowledge of God.

Hope helps us to trust in God no matter what happens. It helps us to trust that God loves us and is always guiding us.

Love helps us to love God, ourselves, and others. We treat all people with respect because God created and loves each person.

We grow in faith, hope, and love by practicing them every day. By making choices to live these virtues, we please God and grow in holiness.

ABOUT
THE BEATITUDES

Jesus taught us the Beatitudes to help us live as witnesses to God's kingdom. When we live the Beatitudes, we help others understand what God wants for all people.

The Beatitudes	Living the Beatitudes
Blessed are the poor in spirit, for theirs is the kingdom of heaven.	We are poor in spirit when we know that we need God more than anything else.
Blessed are they who mourn, for they will be comforted.	We try to help those who are in sorrow or those who are hurting. We know God will comfort them.
Blessed are the meek, for they will inherit the land.	We are gentle and patient with others. We believe we will share in God's promises.
Blessed are they who hunger and thirst for righteousness, for they will be satisfied.	We try to be fair and just toward others. We share what we have with those in need.
Blessed are the merciful, for they will be shown mercy.	We forgive those who are unkind to us. We accept the forgiveness of others.
Blessed are the clean of heart, for they will see God.	We try to keep God first in our lives.
Blessed are the peacemakers, for they will be called children of God.	We try to bring God's peace to the world. When we live peacefully, we are known as God's children.
Blessed are they who are persecuted for the sake of righteousness, for theirs is the kingdom of heaven.	We try to do what is right even when we are teased or insulted. We believe we will be with God forever.

Based on Matthew 5:3–10

THE COMMANDMENTS

The Ten Commandments are God's Laws of love. God gave us the Commandments as a gift to help us live in peace. Jesus told us that we must always obey the Commandments.

The Ten Commandments	Living the Ten Commandments
1. I am the LORD your God. You shall not have other gods besides me.	We believe in God. We only worship God. We love him more than everyone and everything else. We offer God prayers of adoration and of thanksgiving.
2. You shall not take the name of the LORD, your God, in vain.	We never use the name of God or Jesus in an angry way. We use the names of God, Jesus, Mary, and the saints with respect at all times.
3. Remember to keep holy the Sabbath day.	On Sunday we honor God in special ways. We worship him by attending Mass with our family and friends.
4. Honor your father and mother.	We love, honor, respect, and obey our parents and all adults who care for us.
5. You shall not kill.	We believe that God gives us the gift of life. We must protect the lives of children not yet born, the sick, and the elderly. We respect the life and health of others. We must live peacefully and prevent harm from coming to ourselves and others.
6. You shall not commit adultery.	God created man and woman in his image. God calls each to accept his or her identity. The Church teaches that chastity is important for us to be healthy and happy. We must respect our bodies and the bodies of others. We honor the lifelong marriage covenant.
7. You shall not steal.	We take good care of the gifts that God has given us and share them with others. We want others who come after us to have them, too. We do not cheat.
8. You shall not bear false witness against your neighbor.	We must not tell lies, or mislead others on purpose. We must not hurt others by what we say. If we have misled somebody, then we must correct what we have said.
9. You shall not covet your neighbor's wife.	We respect the promises married people have made to each other. We must always dress and act in a decent way.
10. You shall not covet anything that belongs to your neighbor.	We are satisfied with what we have. We are not jealous, envious, or greedy. The Gospel teaches us to place God first in our lives.

Based on Exodus 20:2–17

God's Laws for Today

When God created the world, he gave people two commands—take care of the world he created and build the human family. When God gave us the Ten Commandments through Moses, he did so to remind us that his Laws are based on the nature of creation.

And so we follow the Fifth Commandment when we protect all that God created, especially human life. Attacking human life in the form of an innocent, unborn child (abortion) or as a sick or elderly person (euthanasia) is against God's Law because it is against God's creation.

The Church believes that the family is at the heart of the human community. And so the Sixth Commandment teaches that husbands and wives must be faithful to each other for life. Families welcome children and help them grow.

God created people in his own image. Because of this, the Eighth Commandment requires us to always be truthful as God is truth.

At creation, God asked us to increase and multiply and care for the Earth. We are reminded of this responsibility when we think about God's Commandments.

The Great Commandment

Jesus told us that the Ten Commandments could be summed up in what is known as the Great Commandment. "Love God with all your heart, with all your mind, and with all your strength, and love your neighbor as yourself" (based on Mark 12:30–31).

The New Commandment

Jesus told us that besides giving us the Great Commandment, he wanted to give us the New Commandment. The New Commandment Jesus gave us is, "Love one another as I love you" (based on John 15:12).

Jesus' love for us is the perfect example of how to live. When we love others and treat them as Jesus taught us, we live in happiness and freedom.

ABOUT
VOCATIONS
Many Ways of Serving

Laypersons Most Catholics live out their baptismal vocation as **laypersons**. Laypersons usually hold jobs in society and are either single or married. As part of their Christian vocation, laypersons often volunteer their time and skills in serving their local parish community or diocese. They may help care for the poor, teach as a catechist in religious education classes, help with parish organizations, or invite others to join the Church. In these and many other ways, laypersons help the parish community fulfill its mission to reach out to all in the spirit of Jesus.

Religious Sisters and Brothers Some men and women choose to devote their entire lives to the ministry of the Catholic Church. These people join religious communities of sisters or brothers. Vows, or promises, of poverty, chastity, and obedience are taken so that the sisters or brothers can be completely devoted to their ministries and become closer to God in community. Each religious community chooses a particular ministry, such as teaching, working with the poor, preaching, prayer and contemplation, nursing work, or parish work.

Ordained Ministers In the Catholic Church, there are also ordained ministers—bishops, priests, and deacons. Baptized men who are called to ordained ministry have the special vocation of leading the community in worship, as well as serving in a wide variety of ministries within the Church.

Bishops are the chief teachers of the faith. They administer dioceses and celebrate Sacraments.

Diocesan priests serve in positions such as pastors of parishes, educators, and counselors. Priests who belong to religious communities may be assigned as pastors or teachers, or they may work in the particular ministry of their communities.

Most deacons that serve in parishes are called "permanent deacons." These men usually assist the pastor of a parish by leading the celebrations of Baptism and Marriage, preaching at Sunday Mass, and helping with parish management. Unlike priests, permanent deacons can be married and have families.

HOW CATHOLICS PRAY

When we pray, we are expressing our faith in God. As Catholics, we can pray privately by ourselves. We can also pray with others in the Church community when we gather to worship.

ABOUT
PRAYER

Prayer is listening and talking to God. We can pray to praise and thank God. We pray to ask God for special blessings for ourselves and for others. We can pray to express sorrow for our sins. Sometimes we call upon Mary or one of the saints to pray to God for us.

We believe God always hears our prayers. We believe God always answers our prayers in the way that is best for us. Jesus said, "Whatever you ask the Father in my name, he will give you" (based on John 16:23).

ABOUT
THE KINDS OF PRAYER

Just as we have different ways of talking and listening to our friends, we have different ways of praying.

It is always possible to pray. We can pray without saying words. When we are quiet and we think about God, we are praying. This is a very good way to pray because the Holy Spirit speaks to our hearts. Another way to pray is to quietly think about a Bible story. We can try to imagine ourselves being in the crowd when Jesus preached. This kind of prayer helps us to think about what our faith means to us. We can also use church music or instrumental music to help us pray. Music can help us focus on prayer when it is easy to get distracted.

Beautiful sights in nature remind us of God's wonderful gifts. When we see a sunrise or sunset, smell the ocean or a flower, see the colored leaves in autumn, or even play with our pets, we can pray a quiet prayer of thanks to God.

THE LORD'S PRAYER

Jesus taught his followers to pray. He gave us the Lord's Prayer so that we can honor God and remember God's love for us. This prayer teaches us many important lessons about how God wants us to live.

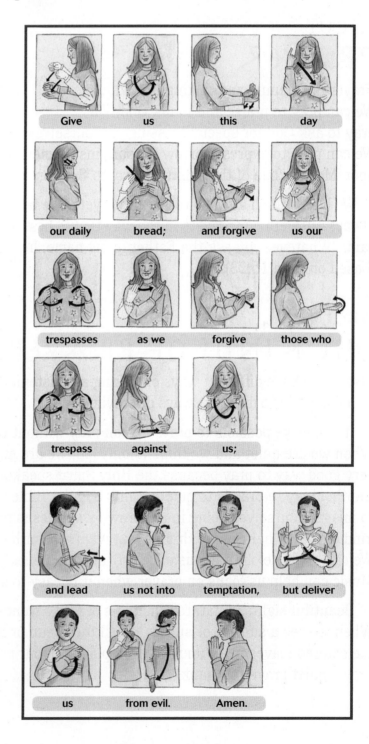

The Lord's Prayer

Our Father, who art in heaven, hallowed be thy name;

God is our Father. We praise and thank God for all the wonderful gifts he has given us. We pray that God's name will be spoken with respect and reverence at all times.

thy kingdom come,

Jesus told us about God's kingdom in Heaven. We pray that everyone will live as Jesus teaches us to live. We look forward to the day when God's kingdom will finally come.

thy will be done on earth as it is in heaven.

We pray that everyone will obey God's Laws. We know that Jesus has taught us how to live as his followers. We wish to show others how to live as Christians.

Give us this day our daily bread,

God cares for us. We know that we can pray for our needs. We know that we must pray for the needs of the poor. We ask God for the good things we can share with others.

and forgive us our trespasses,
as we forgive those who trespass against us;

We ask God for forgiveness when we have done something wrong. We forgive those who have hurt us.

and lead us not into temptation,

We pray that God will help us make good choices and do what is right. When we have difficult choices to make, we can pray to the Holy Spirit for guidance.

but deliver us from evil.

We pray that God will protect us from what is harmful. We know that we should care for our own health and the well-being of others.

Amen.

When we say "Amen," it means "I believe."

Glossary

Abraham God chose Abraham to bring his sacred Covenant to the Hebrew people. *(page 49)*

absolution Absolution is the prayer and declaration of forgiveness for sins prayed by the priest in the Sacrament of Penance and Reconcilation. *(page 165)*

anointed Being anointed means that a person has a special mission. We are anointed with holy oil when we are baptized and confirmed. *(page 81)*

Anointing of the Sick Anointing of the Sick is the Sacrament of Healing that brings Jesus' comfort to people who are very sick, old, or near death. *(page 264)*

Ascension The Ascension is the moment when Jesus, in his resurrected body, entered Heaven. *(page 71)*

assembly An assembly is a gathering of Catholics to celebrate the Eucharist and other Sacraments. *(page 206)*

Baptism Baptism is the Sacrament of Initiation that welcomes us into the Church and frees us from all sin. *(page 80)*

Beatitudes The Beatitudes are Jesus' teachings about how to live and find real happiness in God's kingdom. *(page 90)*

bishop A bishop is the leader of a diocese. Bishops are the chief teachers of the Catholic Church. *(page 122)*

Bible The Bible is the Word of God. The Holy Spirit guided people to write all that is contained in the Bible. *(page 28)*

Blessed Sacrament The Blessed Sacrament is another name for the Eucharist. *(page 143)*

Body of Christ The Body of Christ is the People of God or the Church. *(page 155)*

Chrism Chrism is perfumed oil that has been blessed by the bishop. *(page 81)*

Christ's mission Christ's mission is to bring the Kingdom of God to all people. The Church guides us in spreading God's peace and love to the world. *(page 154)*

Communion of Saints The Communion of Saints is the community of all people, living and dead, who believe in Jesus Christ. *(page 197)*

Confirmation Confirmation is the Sacrament of Initiation in which the Holy Spirit strengthens our faith and helps us become fuller members of the Church. *(page 122)*

conscience Our conscience is our ability to know what is good and what is wrong. God speaks to us in our conscience and helps us make responsible decisions. *(page 175)*

Corporal Works of Mercy The Corporal Works of Mercy are the loving actions by which we respond to the basic physical needs of people. *(page 217)*

covenant A covenant is an agreement between persons or groups of people. God made a special Covenant with his people. *(page 49)*

deacon A deacon is a person who is ordained to serve the parish community in many ways. *(page 265)*

divine Divine means "of God." Jesus Christ is both human and divine—that is, both a human being and God. *(page 71)*

Eucharist The Eucharist is the Sacrament of the Body and Blood of Jesus Christ. *(page 38)*

examination of conscience An examination of conscience is deciding whether our words and actions show love for God and others. *(page 133)*

faith Faith is belief and trust in God. *(page 59)*

Gifts of the Holy Spirit The Gifts of the Holy Spirit are wisdom, understanding, knowledge, right judgment, courage, reverence, and wonder and awe. These gifts help us know and love God and live as his followers. *(page 122)*

Gospel Gospel means "Good News." At Mass we hear readings about Jesus' life and teachings from the four Gospels in the New Testament. *(page 207)*

grace Grace is God's life within us that fills us with his love. *(page 122)*

Holy Orders Holy Orders is the Sacrament in which bishops, priests, and deacons are ordained to serve the Church. *(page 197)*

Holy Trinity The Holy Trinity is One God in Three Persons. The Three Persons are God the Father, God the Son, and God the Holy Spirit. *(page 29)*

homily A homily is a talk a priest or deacon gives to help us understand God's message in the Gospel and other readings. *(page 207)*

immersed Immersed means being placed in water for Baptism. *(page 80)*

justice Justice means treating everyone fairly and with respect by following Jesus' teachings. *(page 100)*

Kingdom of God The Kingdom of God is God's promise of justice, peace, and joy that all his people will share at the end of time. *(page 59)*

Law of Love The Law of Love is the loving message in which Jesus united the Ten Commandments and the Beatitudes into one. It is also known as the New Commandment. *(page 133)*

layperson A layperson is any Catholic except bishops, priests, or deacons. *(page 274)*

Liturgy of the Eucharist The Liturgy of the Eucharist is the part of the Mass in which the bread and wine are changed into the Body and Blood of Christ. *(page 39)*

Liturgy of the Word The Liturgy of the Word is the part of the Mass in which we hear the Word of God in the Scriptures. *(page 39)*

Mass The Mass is the celebration of the Eucharist. *(page 38)*

Matrimony Matrimony is the Sacrament that celebrates the covenant between a man and a woman. *(page 265)*

mercy Mercy is the loving kindness that God shows to sinners. *(page 59)*

monastery A monastery is a place where members of a religious community live. *(page 30)*

moral decisions Moral decisions are choices between what is good and what is wrong. *(page 175)*

mortal sin A mortal sin is a serious violation of God's law. It separates us from God's grace until we ask for forgiveness in the Sacrament of Penance and Reconciliation. *(page 164)*

mystery A mystery is what cannot be understood about God. *(page 30)*

New Commandment The New Commandment is the loving message in which Jesus united the Ten Commandments and the Beatitudes into one. It is also known as the Law of Love. *(page 133)*

Noah Noah is the person whom God promised that he would never again destroy the world by flood. God's promise to Noah was a covenant, or agreement, with all living beings. *(page 49)*

Original Sin Original Sin is the sin of Adam and Eve that has been passed on to all human beings. Because of this, we are weakened in our ability to resist sin and to do good. *(page 81)*

parable A parable is a story that teaches a moral or religious lesson. Parables use everyday events and objects to explain important truths. *(page 185)*

Paschal Mystery The Paschal Mystery is the suffering, Death, Resurrection, and Ascension of Jesus Christ. We are united to Jesus' Paschal Mystery in the Sacraments. *(page 71)*

peace Peace is the calm, good feeling of being together with God and with others. Peace follows forgiveness. *(page 185)*

Penance and Reconciliation Penance and Reconciliation is the Sacrament of Healing that celebrates the gift of God's love and forgiveness. *(page 164)*

Pentecost Pentecost is the day on which Jesus sent the gift of the Holy Spirit to his first disciples. This event marks the beginning of the Church. *(page 113)*

petition A petition is a prayer in which we ask for God's forgiveness and help. Petition is one of the four kinds of prayer. *(page 227)*

priest A priest is a person called by God to lead the community in worship and to serve in a wide variety of ministries in the Church. *(page 39)*

role models Role models are people who show us how to bring God's goodness into the world by their example. *(page 69)*

Rosary The Rosary is a special devotion that honors Mary, the Mother of God and Jesus. The Rosary helps us to meditate on events in the lives of Jesus and Mary. *(page 15)*

Sacraments Sacraments are sacred signs that celebrate God's love for us and Jesus' presence in our lives and in the Church. *(page 155)*

Sacraments at the Service of Communion The Sacraments at the Service of Communion are Holy Orders and Matrimony. These two Sacraments celebrate two special ways that people serve God by sharing their gifts with others. *(page 265)*

Sacraments of Healing The Sacraments of Healing are Penance and Reconciliation and Anointing of the Sick. *(page 264)*

Sacraments of Initiation The Sacraments of Initiation are Baptism, Confirmation, and Eucharist. *(page 123)*

sacred Sacred means something that comes from God. *(page 262)*

sacred images Sacred images are statues or pictures that remind us of God, Mary, and the saints. *(page 50)*

Scripture Scripture is the written Word of God that we read in the Bible. *(page 18)*

sin A sin is any thought, word, or action that turns us away from God's Law. *(page 164)*

Spiritual Works of Mercy The Spiritual Works of Mercy are loving actions that respond to people's basic spiritual needs. *(page 217)*

tabernacle A tabernacle is the special container in church where the Blessed Sacrament is kept for personal prayer and for distribution to those unable to come to Mass due to illness. *(page 143)*

Ten Commandments The Ten Commandments are the laws God gave to Moses. They help us live in peace by loving God, ourselves, and others. *(page 48)*

venial sin A venial sin is a less serious sin. It weakens our love for God and others and can lead to mortal sin. *(page 164)*

vocation A vocation is the work we do as members of the Church. We are called to use our talents to carry on Christ's mission in the world. *(page 197)*

worship To worship is to give honor and praise to God, especially as a community. *(page 50)*

Index

A

Abraham, 49
Absolution, 165, 264, 269
Act of Contrition, 14
Adoration, 146, 148
Advent, 234–236, 243–244
Adultery, 48, 272
Alleluia, 254
Amen, 277
American Sign Language, 61–62, 82, 103–104, 145, 187, 229, 276
Angels, 216, 258
Anointed, 81, 122–123, 262–263, 264
Anointing of the Sick, 264
Apostles, 18, 206, 260–261
  See also Disciples.
Apostles' Creed, The, 12, 14
Ascension, 71, 113, 71, 112–113, 234–236
Assembly, 206–207
Ave, Maria (prayer), 11

B

Baptism, 80–81, 84, 112, 122–123, 262, 154, 197, 122–124, 220, 226, 254, 262–263, 274
Beatitudes, 90–94, 101, 102, 216–217, 270, 271
Benedict XVI (pope), 204
Bible, 18–20, 28–30, 186, 218, 258, 260, 269
Bishops, 104, 122–123, 197, 263, 265, 267, 274
Blessed Sacrament, 143, 146
Body and Blood of Christ, 39, 123, 207, 263, 268
Body of Christ (Church), 122, 154–155, 158, 188, 208

C

Catholic Church, 84, 113, 155, 164–166, 176, 206–207, 244–245, 248, 251–252, 256, 257–258, 261
  apostolic role of, 154, 261
  as Body of Christ, 122
  community of, 42, 80–81, 84, 155, 165, 236
  guidance of, 49, 236
  leadership of, 104, 261
  Marks of the, 261

teachings of, 30, 121, 124, 133, 175, 258, 260–261
  See also Liturgy and Worship.
Catholics
  community of, 40, 104, 123, 207, 265
  living as, 206
  mission of, 195
  and prayer, 241–242
  responsibilities of, 49, 227, 236
  worship by, 252, 257–258
Chrism, 81, 123
Christians, 18, 70–71, 81, 104, 131, 133, 142, 153–155, 164–165, 197, 207, 225, 227, 248, 252, 254, 265
Christmas, 72, 234–236, 244–245
Christ's mission, 154–155, 195, 197
Church, 29, 50, 80, 143, 248, 254
Communion, 143, 252, 263
  See also Eucharist.
Communion of Saints, 84, 197, 207
Confirmation, 122–124, 197, 263
Conscience, 133, 168, 175, 270
Corporal Works of Mercy, 217–219
Courage, 121, 123–124, 126, 142–143, 256
Covenant, 49, 102, 133
Creation, 28–30, 124, 168, 254, 273
Crucifixion, 70, 84, 146

D

Deacons, 80–81, 197, 248, 262–263, 265, 274
Disciples, 49, 112–113, 122, 132, 216, 226, 256
Divine, 71

E

Easter, 234–236, 252–254
Easter candle, 81
Easter Sunday, 252–254
Easter Vigil, 234–235, 251–252, 254
Egypt, 48
Eighth Commandment, 48–50, 52, 175, 185–186, 272–273
Eucharist, 38–40, 123, 143, 206–208, 210, 251–252, 263
Evil, 134, 227, 229, 250, 277
Examination of conscience, 133, 168, 264

F

Faith, 59, 84, 122, 142–143, 206–207, 210, 227, 230, 236, 259
Feast days, 234–235
  the Baptism of the Lord, 234–235
  the Holy Family, 234–235
Fifth Commandment, 48–50, 52, 133–134, 144, 272–273
First Commandment, 48–52, 59–60, 272–273
Forgiveness, 70, 84, 113, 164–166, 168, 173–175, 178, 183–188, 227, 264
Fourth Commandment, 48–49, 52, 133–134, 144, 272–273

G

Gabriel (angel), 258
Galilee, 226
Gifts of the Holy Spirit, 121–124
Glózia Patzi, 10
Glory Be, 10
God, 18, 27–30, 32, 37–40, 42, 47–50, 52, 57–60, 69–71, 74, 79–81, 84, 89–94, 100–102, 112–113, 116, 121–124, 133, 136, 141–144, 153–155, 163–166, 168, 173–175, 178, 195–198, 200, 205–207, 215–217, 220, 225–228, 238, 242, 246, 249–250, 257–258, 260, 264
Good Friday, 234–235, 251–252
Gospel, 59, 207, 230, 267
Grace, 122–123, 155, 164–165, 250, 261, 264
Great Commandment, 273
Green, Nicholas, 134

H

Hail, Holy Queen, 14
Hail Mary, 11
Happiness, 89–91, 133
Heaven, 58, 62, 71, 81, 112, 143, 210, 244, 249, 258
Hebrews, 48–50, 60, 133
Holy Communion, 39–40

Holy days of obligation, 18, 49, 236
Holy Land (map), 21
Holy Orders, 197, 265
Holy Saturday, 251–252
Holy Spirit, 29–30, 32, 39, 59, 71,
    80–81, 84, 111–113, 116, 121–
    124, 126, 256
    and Pentecost, 112–113, 116,
        234–235
    and the Sacraments, 39, 80–81,
        123, 155, 165, 207, 226,
        263–264
    and Scripture writers, 18, 29, 260
    symbols of, 112, 256
Holy Thursday, 234–235, 251–252
Holy Trinity, 29–30, 71, 84, 133,
    246, 260
Holy water, 80, 254
Holy Week, 235
Homily, 207, 265, 267
Hope, 259

I

Immersed, 80, 263
Intercession, 116

J

Jerusalem, 256
Jesus Christ, 18, 29, 39–40, 42,
    49–50, 58–60, 69–72, 74,
    80–81, 84, 90–92, 94, 100–101,
    104, 112–113, 116, 122–124,
    132–133, 136, 142–143, 146,
    154–156, 164–166, 174, 176,
    184–185, 188, 195–198, 200,
    210, 215–217, 220, 226,
    234–236, 242, 246, 248–252,
    254, 256, 258, 260, 263
Jews, 112, 256
    See also Hebrews.
John XXII (pope), 30
John Paul II (pope, Blessed), 134,
    204
Justice, 91, 100–101, 104, 142,
    197–198, 206, 225, 227, 244, 250

K

Kingdom of God, 59, 90–94, 99,
    101, 104, 146, 154–155, 184,
    197, 216, 244
Knowledge, 121, 123–124

L

Last Supper, 216, 234–235
Law of Love, 133, 216–217,
    227–228
    See also New Commandment.
Laying on of hands, 122–123, 263
Laypersons, 248, 274
Lent, 235, 247–250
Litany of Saints, 210
Liturgical year, 234–236
Liturgy, 207
Liturgy of the Eucharist, 39, 42,
    268
Liturgy of the Word, 39, 268
Lord's Prayer, The, 10, 58–62, 91,
    101, 103–104, 143, 185, 187–
    188, 229–230, 268, 276–277
Love, 49, 59–60, 71, 91, 101–102,
    113, 116, 123, 131–134,
    141–143, 146, 154–155,
    163–164, 166, 168, 173–175,
    178, 195, 197, 200, 206–207,
    210, 215–217, 227, 230, 240,
    248, 250, 270

M

Magi, 246
Marriage, 134, 274
    See also Matrimony.
Mary (Mother of God), 50, 71–72,
    84, 112, 139, 142, 146, 206, 210,
    234–235, 238, 241–242, 244,
    246, 257–258, 261
Mass, 18, 38–40, 49, 71, 101, 143,
    178, 206–207, 236, 246,
    251–252, 254, 266–268, 263
Matrimony, 265
Mercy, 59, 90, 142, 165, 178, 197,
    206–207, 210, 216
Miraculous Medal of Mary, 241–242
Monastery, 30
Moral decisions, 175
Mortal sin, 164
Moses, 48–49, 133
Mystery, 30, 155

N

New Commandment, 132–133,
    216, 273
New Testament, 18, 260
Nicene Creed, The, 13, 267
Ninth Commandment, 48–50, 52,
    175, 185–186, 272–273
Noah, 49

O

Old Testament, 18, 260
Oratio Dominica, 11
Ordinary Time, 234–235
Original Sin, 81

P

Parable, 185
Parish ministries
    altar servers, 44
    Anointing of the Sick and
        ministry to the infirmed, 170
    catechists, 54, 274
    Cursillo movement, 76
    Eucharistic Holy Hour, 148
    extraordinary ministers of
        Holy Communion, 212
    Godparents, 86
    good stewards, 34
    Holy Name Society, 96
    lector, 190
    liturgy committee, 160
    ministries to the poor, 222
    ministries to the unemployed, 202
    music, 64
    parish pastoral council, 180
    parish staff, 106
    RCIA, 128, 220
    Rosary Altar Society, 232
    respect life, 138
    youth ministers, 118
Paschal Mystery, 71
Peace, 49, 91, 154, 165, 168, 178,
    185, 197–198, 225, 227, 230,
    244, 250
Penance and Reconciliation, 164–
    166, 175, 264, 269
Pentecost, 112–113, 122, 234–235,
    255–256
Petition, 52, 227
Prayer, 32, 38, 39, 42, 52, 58–60,
    62, 74, 94, 101–102, 104, 116,
    121, 123, 126, 136, 142–143,
    146, 158, 165, 168, 175, 178,
    185, 197, 200, 206–207, 210,
    217, 220, 225, 227, 230,
    241–242, 248–250, 259
Prayer Before a Crucifix, 200
Prayer to Jesus Christ in the
    Eucharist, 14
Prayer to the Holy Spirit, 126
Priests, 39–40, 42, 80–81,
    164–166, 197, 207, 234–235,
    240, 248, 262–265, 269, 274
Promised Land, 48

R

Religious brothers, 240, 274
Religious communities, 197, 274
 Carmelites, 97, 102
 Daughters of Charity, 213, 242
 Dominicans, 25, 30, 129, 240
 Franciscans, 55, 223
 Little Sisters of the Poor, 130
 Mercedarians, 181
 Missionaries of Charity, 238
 Missionaries of the Sacred Heart, 151
 Poor Clares, 67, 72
 Redemptorists, 203
Religious sisters, 274
Resurrection, 71, 80, 84, 165, 206–207, 220, 226, 234–236, 252, 256, 263
Revelation, 260
Reverence, 121, 123–124
Right judgment, 121, 123–124
Role models, 69, 71, 258
Rosary, The, 15, 36

S

Sabbath, 48, 50
Sacrament, 71, 146, 155–156, 164–165, 207, 262
Sacraments at the Service of Communion, 265
Sacraments of Healing, 165, 264
Sacraments of Initiation, 123, 262
Sacred, 49, 59, 134, 262
Sacred images, 50, 242
Sacrifice, 39, 200, 207, 248
Saints and holy people, 50, 102, 206, 210, 234–235, 241, 261
 Alphonsus Liguori, 203
 Augustine, 210
 Catherine Labouré, 242
 Catherine of Bologna, 67, 72
 Clare, 210
 Francis, 210
 Francis Solano, 109
 John the Baptist, 77
 John Vianney, 161, 166, 210
 Joseph, 206, 210, 244, 246
 Junípero Serra, Blessed, 223
 Justa, 45
 Louis IX, 193, 198
 Louise de Marillac, 213
 Margaret of Castello, 129
 Mariana of Jesus, 181
 Martin de Porres, 240
 Mary (Mother of God), 50, 71–72, 84, 112, 139, 142, 146, 206, 210, 234–235, 238, 241–242, 244, 246, 257–258, 261
 Matilda, 171
 Matthew, 87
 Monica, 210
 Paul, 18, 119, 154, 188
 Peter, 184–185
 Peter of Alcantara, 55
 Pius V, 30
 Pius X, 35, 40
 Rose Philippine Duchesne, 151
 Teresa of Ávila, 55, 74, 97, 102, 210
 Teresa of Calcutta, Blessed, 238
 Thomas Aquinas, 25, 30
Salvation, 146, 178, 207, 249
Schweitzer, Albert, 218
Scripture, 39–40, 71, 94, 175, 186, 246, 256, 260, 263
Scripture stories,
 creation, 28
 Jesus and his family, 142
 one Body, many parts, 154
 Pentecost, 112
 seeing Christ in others, 216
 the Beatitudes, 90–91
 the commissioning of the disciples, 226
 the Crucifixion, 70–71
 the forgiving father, 174
 the laborers in the vineyard, 100
 the light of the world, 196
 the Lord's Prayer, 58–59
 the New Commandment, 132
 the Ten Commandments, 48–49
 the unforgiving servant, 184
Second Commandment, 48–50, 59–60, 272–273
Seventh Commandment, 48–50, 52, 175, 185–186, 272–273
Sign of the Cross, The, 10, 123, 220, 264, 266, 268
Signum Crucis, 10
Sin, 80, 133, 164–165, 174–175, 227
 forgiveness of, 84, 178, 184, 252, 264
 mortal, 164
 Original, 81
 Salvation from, 39, 71, 123, 206, 210
 sorrow for, 186
 venial, 164
Sixth Commandment, 48–50, 52, 133–134, 144, 272–273
Solemnities
 the Ascension of the Lord, 234–235
 the Assumption of the Blessed Virgin Mary, 257–258
 the Most Holy Body and Blood of Christ, 234–235
 Pentecost Sunday 255–256
 the Most Holy Trinity 234–235
Son of God, 122, 200, 216
Son of Man, 216
Spiritual Works of Mercy, 217, 219
Stations of the Cross, The, 16, 248
Sunday, 18, 38, 49, 71, 206, 234–236, 254

T

Tabernacle, 143
Ten Commandments, 48–50, 52, 60, 91, 93, 101–102, 133–134, 141–144, 175, 185, 216–217, 227–228, 272–273
Tenth Commandment, 48–50, 52, 175, 185–186, 272–273
Third Commandment, 48–50, 59–60, 272–273
Tradition, 260
Triduum, 251–252

U

Understanding, 121, 123–124, 143

V

Venial sin, 164
Virtues, 270
 See also Faith, Hope, *and* Love.
Vocation Prayer, 14
Vocations, 197, 200, 274

W

Way of the Cross, 248
Wisdom, 121, 123–124
Wonder and awe, 121, 123–124
Word of God (Scripture), 18, 39, 260
Worship, 18, 50, 60, 102, 146
 See also Liturgy and Mass.